The Charge Is
RAPE

The Charge Is

RAPE

by Gerald Astor

PLAYBOY PRESS

Contents

The Charge Is
RAPE

I

Preface to Rape

Rape: a subject for jokes, boys and men giggling on the front stoop, scuffling in the schoolyard dust, swapping lies in the saloon. "Did you hear about the girl I saved from rape last night? Yeah, I changed my mind." "Rape is impossible," say Confucious. "Girl can run faster with skirts up than man with pants down." "When rape is inevitable, lie back and enjoy it." "There once was a maid from Dundee, who was raped by an ape in a tree. . . ." Or Ogden Nash: "Seduction is for sissies; the he-man likes his rape."

Lots of laughs. A woman, forced off the street at knifepoint, is led into a garbage-strewn alley, broken bricks for a pillow, while the would-be lover rips away her clothes. Or, the husband sits bound and gagged in the bedroom while the trio of burglars, with only their eyes visible through the knitted masks, ravishes the wife, forces her to commit fellatio. In the dental chair, the anesthetized patient dreams a peculiar vision, that the practitioner has filled her mouth with his penis rather than with dental tools. She awakens to stains upon her blouse, a pungent odor. On a rooftop, naked, a woman has been waiting for help since, six hours previous, the man in the elevator showed her the dark round hole mouth of a pistol. In her automobile, the good samaritan attempts to shake off the pain from the gash on her head, a love tribute offered by the man to whom she offered a ride. In the psychiatrist's office, the patient hesitates as again the series of sexual assaults by her brother intrudes upon her consciousness. Out on the highway, the bloody nosed date searches for a taxi and resolves no more singles bars. Free at last from the trunk of the car, nose and skull fractured, the former virgin knows not of the caked blood between her legs, her initiation to the ranks of "womanhood," the favor of a sponsor who had tracked her for days.

"Rape, carnal knowledge of a woman against her will or without her consent" reads the classic definition. Knowledge indeed. In a court of law that skimpy meeting, that brief moment of touching, the intrusion of the temporarily proud male flesh, may constitute "knowledge." But does that mean to *know* another human being? That brief, unlawful invasion, can that encompass a study of the entire body, the chemistry, the mind of another individual? The rapist knows the woman as well as the murderer whose bullet penetrates flesh "knows" his victim.

Behind the act flickers a male fantasy of sexual alchemy; the turd of lust turns into a golden shower of mutual passion. The few seconds of heave and spasm, the host passive in the presence of the invader; somehow the bearer of an unwelcome gift flatters himself that once bestowed it magically transforms itself, toad into butterfly. Yes, she loved it, really desired it, that quick brutal pop. Yes it made the barren become fruitful. Yes, just as a great arid valley turns a verdant green when the dam finally breaks and is followed by a tiny puddle, it is the best that man can master.

But art pretends to higher truths than life. *Straw Dogs, Blume in Love, The Man Who Loved Cat Dancing, Pat Garrett and Billy the Kid, The Getaway* offer rape as cinematic revelation and triumph of the human spirit. Jack Valenti's office rated the films *R* or *X*. But the ticket hustlers knew that rape, like the murder of a president, fascinates while it repels. There are some limits to the vicarious joys of the public, however. *Clockwork's* Alex, the old "in and out" fella, in the book ravished a pair of naughty preteens. In the flick, it became a stutter speed rape of two, well-postpubescent dollies, a regular laugher. But why focus upon the most recent form of exploitation? From Chaucer to Updike, rape has been seen as an up.

Meanwhile, a gathering of women, no longer muttering retreats, takes to the streets, to the hearing rooms, to the basements of churches. "Rape is a political crime," cry some. Arrest, convict and lock up the rapists. Put 'em away, the handful of innocents who suffer, along with the guilty. The streets, the homes, must be freed. "The persistent threat of rape," one more male instrument to keep women under the yoke that threatens the freedom of all women, must be exterminated.

Note: In all cases, the names of the victims have been disguised.

II

Cops and the Crime

A male is guilty of rape in the first degree when he engages in sexual intercourse with a female under any of the following circumstances:

1. By forcible compulsion (see definition under "Consent").

2. The female is incapable of consent by reason of being physically helpless (see definition under "Consent").

3. The female is less than 11.

Rape first is a Class B Felony.

—FROM *The New York State Criminal Law Code*

In the fall of 1973, a 22-year-old woman—I will call her Brenda Adams—arrived in New York City to visit her parents who lived in Brooklyn. Employed as an airline-reservation clerk in Kansas City, Brenda Adams was described as "nothing beautiful, but a really good body." On this particular trip to New York, Brenda Adams telephoned an acquaintance named Sally Clark, whom she had met casually at a roller-skating rink. Sally Clark invited Brenda Adams to join her and a couple of friends at a quiet party in Harlem.

From Harlem, a foursome of the two young women and two men went on to another apartment, this time in the South Bronx. Music was pouring out of a stereo system when Brenda Adams noticed that a number of her companions were sniffing cocaine. "I should have known then that I should leave," said the airlines clerk. But she remained.

About this time, Sally Clark announced that she wanted to get a pack of cigarettes at a nearby store. She left the party and as time slipped by, it became apparent that she would not return. In the apartment, two men began to molest Brenda Adams, pawing at her, soliciting her to retreat to the bedroom with them. She refused.

Resistance only seemed to infuriate the two men. With no protest from the few other people in the apartment, the pair shoved Brenda Adams out the door and hauled her up two flights of stairs and out onto the roof. There was even less patience with the young woman once she was isolated on the roof. With a belt from her raincoat, the men tied her hands. In full terror now, Brenda Adams, who until this moment could not believe what was about to happen, began to scream.

The noise attracted tenants living on the top floor. A head poked up through the door to the roof. The spectator observed the struggling figures for a moment and then vanished. Within a minute or two, a police siren ripped through the night air and reached the ears of those atop the five-story building. The two men quickly dragged the young woman back down the stairs and into the apartment. The man who actually lived in the apartment flashed a pistol, "Girl, if you make a sound you get the first bullet."

From outside of the apartment door came the sound of feet, cop feet, slapping on the stairs. They could be heard climbing to the top floor of the apartment where the police canvassed the tenants, asking who had called them and then searching for any young woman in trouble. Brenda Adams waited a floor below, not knowing whether or not to hope. Finally, the patrolmen could be heard going down the stairs to make their radio report that they had found nothing. When it seemed certain that they were gone the resident of the apartment growled to the two would-be attackers, "Get her the hell out of here."

They hustled Brenda Adams down to the street and shoved her into an automobile. It was 10 o'clock at night and only the start of a brutal evening. The car wandered through the streets of the city, seemingly aimless, while one of the men went through the contents of the young woman's pocketbook. Brenda Adams never heard their full names, knew them only by the way they addressed one another, "Connie" and "Stubbs."

From the purse, Stubbs extracted a letter from

7

Brenda's mother to her. On the envelope Mrs. Adams had written her Brooklyn address. Connie maneuvered the automobile down Manhattan's East Side Drive, over the Williamsburg Bridge and finally braked to a stop in front of the house where the parents lived.

"Girl, we know where your family lives. If you go to the police about this, we'll get them." Terrified, the girl could only plead to be freed and protest that she would never make any complaint. But the captors were relentless, alternating threats with cajoles.

The car continued to sift through the streets of the city. Now it moved into the Borough of Queens and Connie parked in a driveway on a quiet street. A random stream of impressions marked Brenda Adams's memory. She registered the crunch of gravel under the tires. Then she was led over a driveway into a one-family house. While Stubbs guarded her in the living room, Connie entered a bedroom and carried on a half-audible conversation with a woman. Stubbs cuffed Brenda Adams and from the woman in the bedroom came a reprieving order, "If you're going to beat her or fuck her, get her outa here."

The trio retreated to the automobile. As the door shut behind them, Brenda Adams's memory recorded the distinctive paint combination on the inside of the kitchen door. Her time had come, however. Connie eased the car into a dark corner of a saloon parking lot. Both men then raped Brenda Adams, penetrating, ejaculating. After a brief respite, Connie forced her to commit fellatio, or sodomy as it is described in the criminal code.

Sated temporarily, the rapists then continued their carnal voyage. On the Throggs Neck Bridge, an airy span that joins Queens to the Bronx, Stubbs pushed Brenda's head down savagely to sodomize her again. On Bruckner Boulevard, one of the major concrete arteries through the heart of the Bronx, Stubbs and Connie decided to get rid of their companion. Dumped out by the side of the road, Brenda Adams received a final warning, "Remember, we know where your mother and father live." They drove off, keeping her pocketbook with its contents, a wallet full of identification cards and $40.

The time was about 2 A.M. The few cars that rushed by hardly paused to notice the staggering young woman. But then Brenda Adams spotted a "gypsy cab," one of the quasilegal hacks that, in New York City, are barred from cruising but which, in fact, supply much of the transportation in the black ghetto— an area that regular licensed or medallion cabs not only don't cruise in, but also try to avoid.

"Please, take me to the police, I've been attacked" pleaded Brenda Adams. With the young woman huddled on the back seat, the driver headed toward the local precinct. When he came abreast of a radio car, however, he turned the young woman over to the patrolmen. They notified headquarters of their new mission, to take a possible rape victim to Lincoln Hospital for treatment.

At Lincoln, a resident gynecologist with a nurse examined the young woman. Television dramatizations called "Cry Rape" in 1973 and "A Case of Rape" in 1974 purported to give documentary views of the indignities piled upon a victim in the first events after rape. Both programs showed a policeman present in the examination room. When the distraught victims, after putting their feet in the stirrups suddenly became aware of his presence, they cried, in effect "What's he doing here?"

The women were informed the cops were required to be present as witnesses. This, of course, is absolute nonsense. By law it is the attending physician who must serve as the witness, along with the inevitable nurse who always stands by when a male physician examines a female patient. The scene of a cop leaning with his back against the door, notebook in hand, waiting while the physician calls out his findings is ludicrous.

The preliminary examination report by the Lincoln Hospital doctor showed that sexual intercourse had indeed occured. Semen was discovered in Brenda Adams's vagina. She was not a virgin, or otherwise there might have been additional admittable evidence of penetration which in court is a weighty piece of evidence for a finding of rape. He examined her rectum for marks of attempted entry or bruises. After collecting from the vaginal pool some semen which would be made into slides for closer study at the police crime laboratory, the gynecologist administered a douche, a hormone shot that painfully but certainly prevents conception and a precautionary shot of penicillin to ward off venereal disease.

The physician also treated Brenda Adams for her lacerated lip, bloodied by one of the numerous slaps to her face. Except for the split lip and some facial bruises, the doctor found no other marks on Brenda Adams, no teeth marks or scraped elbows or thigh contusions, common signs of rape or, for that matter, lawful passion. Nor did he discern any alien hairs on her body or scrapings of flesh under fingernails, such as might be present had she attempted to claw away the attackers.

The patrol car brought Brenda Adams to a Bronx precinct station where she again told her story briefly to a detective. Under a system of specialization, each of New York City's five boroughs was now staffed by a sex crimes unit. Formerly, sex crimes figured as just one more felony in a detective's crime bag. Since sex crimes, for many reasons, have traditionally proven difficult to prove, and perhaps because of male chauvinism, sex crimes under the old system invariably received less attention than burglary, armed robbery, assault and battery or homicide. But members of the sex crimes squad make points in the department only by clearing offenses in their specialty. As a result, when Brenda Adams finally sat down to discuss her case with Detective Thomas Kelly, an 18-year veteran of the force, she met with an individual who was committed to following through.

Although a dingy morning was but a few hours off, Kelly and his partner took Brenda Adams out in a car in hopes of picking up clues while events still tumbled distinctly in her memory. She knew the address of the original building where she had gone to meet Sally Clark. The two detectives drove to that site and Brenda Adams recognized the building. "She was positive that the second place was in Hunts Point," said Tom Kelly. "So we canvassed the area. Eventually, we hit the right street, Longfellow, which she recalled and then she identified the house. We could have gone up to the apartment but the best we could have come up with was the fellow with the gun; that wasn't enough."

As sunlight began to dapple the tatty Bronx tenements, long shadows spread over rubble strewn lots where the remnants of dead buildings lay, and the city began to awaken. For Brenda Adams, the anesthesia of shock wore off, her emotions crashed through. "She broke down, several times," remembered Kelly. "She was really exhausted and kept saying, 'I knew I was in too deep as soon as I saw the coke. I was looking to get out but never got a chance. I felt they would kill me if I didn't submit. The longer they had me, the more I thought they'd kill me.' "

To cap off the night and early morning, the detectives made Polaroid color shots of Brenda Adams's face, recording on film her beaten face, her bloodied lip. In a courtroom it would be evidence of force. If her body had been visibly abused anywhere else, a policewoman would have clicked the camera shutter.

"We drove her home to Brooklyn," said Tom Kelly. "She gave us all her clothes, except her bra. She was missing shoes and the belt of her raincoat. On the clothes were some blood stains. The lab would give us a reading on the blood and any other stains."

Brenda Adams took a day to recover from the trauma of her experience and then returned to the stationhouse for a long interrogation with Kelly. "I told her to tell me everything she could remember that was said. Among the items she could recall was that the guy with the gun in the apartment was called Thomas by others. She remembered that Thomas had bragged about how he beat somebody out of a repair bill on his Oldsmobile; he'd cheated some body and fender shop, after an accident. She also was very sharp on the automobile they drove around in. She said it was a '73 Buick Electra 225, four door black.

"We took another run out to Longfellow Avenue and in the immediate vicinity we discovered three black Oldsmobiles. One of them had a fender that was newly repainted; there was a characteristic dust on it. We ran the license through and it came back as belonging to a guy named Thomas. We checked him out in the BCI [Bureau of Criminal Identification] and he had a record.

"We took her to look at the mug shots and she positively identified him as the guy who pulled the gun. We also went to Con Edison and the phone company to see if Thomas lived in that Longfellow building but those reports came back negative. Brenda Adams described the staircase and landings in the building and from what she told us we were able to determine the actual apartment that she'd been in. It belonged to a girl, but that wasn't much help. All we could hope to get so far was Thomas and his gun.

"Instead of settling for that, I suggested that she work on Sally Clark who had set her up. I said call Sally Clark and say that was some dirty trick she set up. Tell her that you were willing to 'party' but when the guys started to push you around you made up your mind to resist. Tell Sally that you aren't making any complaint but only want your money, driver's license and pocket-book back. We figured that they would feel that if Brenda Adams had gone to the police, we'd be breaking down Thomas's door by now.

"She agreed to make the call but it was a zero; we got no answer from Sally Clark's apartment. Maybe she was scared and had skipped. We decided to spend some time looking for the Buick Electra. We started to canvas Harlem during the night. We found five Buick black Electra 225s. We phoned in the licenses and got the word on who owned them, their age and description. One was registered to a minister, another to some people upstate; none of the owners of these five vehicles fit who we were looking for. Brenda Adams had described one man as gray haired, maybe fifty, the other in his twenties.

"We had her try the call to Sally the next night. Still we drew no answer; it looked like she had really been frightened and was hiding out. Again we cruised through Harlem, looking for that Electra 225. We spotted four more of them. The third one we checked out belonged to a woman in Jamaica [a section in Queens]. That sounded like it might be tied to the house out there where Brenda had been driven from Brooklyn.

"The following afternoon, we took our trip to Jamaica and as we went past the house owned by the woman in whose name the Buick was registered, Brenda broke down. "That's the house, that's the house," she cried. Then she became worried that she might be mistaken, so many of those places look the same. 'If I could see the kitchen door, the pink door with the black trim, I'd be positive.'

"So we parked across the street and waited. After about forty-five minutes, a kid came out the kitchen door. We could see the inside paint, pink with black trim.

"Now we ran a check on the house, the telephone and the car making certain of the identity of the woman listed as owner. There was always the possibility we might pick up something about her male friends from these records. Nothing of value came out of these checks.

"My partner and I, by ourselves, spent the next couple of nights cruising Harlem, looking for our Buick Electra. We spotted the car several times in the neighborhood of two different bars. We felt that the guy hung out at these two places.

"But we still didn't think we had enough to collar anyone. I approached Brenda and asked her if she would put on a Kel set [a miniature recording system.] The idea would be for her to walk up to the guy in the bar, say that she really wasn't mad and then get him to admit in the conversation what he'd done. I had to tell her the facts about the operation, though. She could get hurt. This place she was going to go into was a real bucket of blood; everybody in there was wheeling and dealing. My partner who had been in narcotics knew the joint well. We would have two undercover guys in there to give her protection but still, if all hell broke loose she might be in bad trouble.

"On the other hand, the recording would be invaluable in court. It would be terrific, if she asked him why he took her pocketbook and why he beat her and he gave the answers; we'd have an airtight case. Because, I said, when we go to court, the defense is going to accuse you of being a pross, and the only reason he beat you was because the price wasn't right.

"She agreed without hesitation to wear the Kel. She was a real standup girl, put me one-hundred percent in her corner." Lieutenant Joseph Bausano, Kelly's superior, approved the plan.

The device was installed at a midtown police station. A policewoman assisted Brenda in placing the tiny microphone inside her bra. Because the operation would place her in jeopardy, Brenda Adams was required to waive any claim of injury. That was done right on the tape.

Explained Kelly, "I announce who I am and that activates the tape. I give my name, address, the time, the day that this microphone was put into operation and that its purpose is to engage certain male individuals in conversation in connection with a crime. She then states her name and that she has given permission to record her conversation."

The electronically endowed young woman then met two black plainclothesmen. They would be undercover in the bar. In the event that she would not be able to slip out of the place as the cops moved in for the arrest, she was to turn to them for help. Their mission would be her protection.

The arresting team that would hit the bar, once a satisfactory amount of incriminating conversation had been recorded, included Kelly, his partner, a sergeant and three more detectives.

"Brenda said that she saw only the one gun that Thomas had," said Kelly. "But Stubbs and Connie had threatened to shoot her if she made trouble. In addition, we believed others in that bar might be armed and take action. We took along two shotguns to even the odds.

"We drove to the two locations and struck out at both. There was no sign of our Buick Electra at either place. Meanwhile, Brenda was lying on the floor in the back of the car, covered by a black raincoat. Then we spotted our car heading south on Lenox Avenue and really flying. We felt that sooner or later he would hit a bar. At eleven P.M. we saw him parked in front of a place between 147th and 148th. We backed off half-a-dozen blocks.

"We advised the two black detectives where the place was and they entered the place. She got out of our car and I activated the tape, giving the address of the bar, stating that she would enter, hope to engage the perpetrators in connection with the crime. When she felt that she had enough, she was to go to the bathroom, tell us she was safe and we'd come in and grab the guy. Then we told her where to meet us after it was over.

"She left the car and began to walk toward the bar. The Kel was perfect. We could hear her footsteps on the pavement. A guy asked her for a cigarette, we heard that. She entered the bar, the jukebox was blaring a lot in the background. She went to the bar and ordered a drink. At this point the set went dead.

"We did every damn thing we could to get it going.

Sometimes you can plug it into the lighter in the car to revive it but it was no go. I was ready to throw the thing into the river.

"We decided we'd just have to go up to the bar and get her. Just as we approached the place, we see the Buick pulling away. Ah, to hell with it we said. Let's take him now. We had two cars and we blocked him off, ran up, pulled two fellows out from the front seat. We searched them but they were clean. But meanwhile somebody has seen us in the street with our shotguns and called the police. Everybody in Manhattan North responded. It's a very hairy area, right near where the old Polo Grounds was. [And the site of a double murder of policemen a few years before.]"

Meanwhile, back in that bar, Brenda Adams, after ordering the drink in the last words recorded by her mike saw that the suspect was not present. As agreed she walked to the bathroom and totally unaware of the communications gap or of the brief action outside, reported the situation and advised that she would return to the place where she had left the police car. Brenda Adams confidently strode into the darkness toward the rendezvous point. Upon reaching that location, she found no one, and thinking that perhaps her protectors were a block or so further off continued to walk away from the bar, into a darker and more deserted neighborhood. Into her dead microphone, she whispered softly, "Tom, Tom, I'm back here, but nobody's here, it's going to happen to me again."

Kelly suddenly realized that no one had attended to the star witness. Having seen the prisoners packed off to a stationhouse, he rushed back to the rendezvous point but now Brenda Adams had wandered off. Fortunately, one of the undercovermen had observed her route. He caught up with her before any new disaster could occur.

The farcical episode over, Kelly took Brenda Adams to the stationhouse where she could observe the pair of suspects from behind a one-way looking glass. Brenda Adams positively identified the driver as Connie. His companion, however, meant nothing to her.

Kelly took Connie to an interrogation room, read him his rights and then told him what the rap was. Connie protested, "What's she talking about, she's just a crazy broad."

"We tell him that he's the lesser of two evils, the guy we really want is Stubbs. Connie claims he doesn't know where Stubbs hangs out but that Thomas knows. I says, 'I'll let you call Thomas. I'll be on the extension. All you do is tell Thomas that you're in trouble and that he should come in here.'

"For a while he resists the idea but I tell him, 'You like that Buick? It's a six-thousand-dollar car, air conditioned, stereo, there's a lot of money invested in the car. If you don't cooperate, you'll never see that car again.' He gets very worried and says 'I can't do that.' I tell him, 'You think so, watch me, you'll never see the Buick again, at least not in the shape it was in when we picked you up.'

"Finally, he goes along with calling Thomas. I'm ready. If he says anything wrong, I'll cut him off.

"In half an hour, Thomas shows up with a girl and

another fellow. He tells me that Connie is just the greatest guy in the world and he'd do anything he could to get him out.

"I tell him what Connie's in for and he says, 'She's a crazy broad. She knocked on my door, she wanted a place to pull herself together. But she didn't want to talk to the police. She's only embarrassed because of her family or something.'

"I answer, 'Well, if I can get a statement from Stubbs maybe we can straighten it out. Could you get him in here?'

" 'Sure,' says Thomas, 'I'll go out and get him right now.' "

"I'd like to let you go," the amiable Kelly answered, "But she says you pulled a gun on her. I've got to lock you up on that charge. If you can get me Stubbs, maybe we'll work the whole thing out.

"He asked to use the phone, calls a number and gets Stubbs and says 'Get your ass down between 147 and 148 at the newstand, meet a friend of mine, and don't ask any questions.'

"When Stubbs appears, we arrest him. They were very irate when we put all three under arrest."

Thomas was indicted for kidnapping and possession of a gun. Connie and Stubbs were indicted for first-degree robbery (Brenda Adams's purse with $40 and credit cards), first-degree kidnapping, first-degree rape, first-degree sodomy. It is an imposing set of charges but the case and the ordeal were far from over for Brenda Adams. Arrest begins the judicial procedures. The trial in a rape case can be long and devastating to the chief witness. Six months after the assault, Stubbs and Connie entered not-guilty pleas. Twice they obtained postponements of a trial. "It's now shit or get off the pot," said Kelly in the spring of 1974. "Next time around they either plead guilty or stand trial." The date for a showdown would be late spring, probably.

"You don't get many who are as determined to go all the way with such a thing," said Kelly. "This girl is an exception. Not many you could put a wire on and send into a bar in that neighborhood. Ninety-nine percent of the victims won't go as far. But we still have to prove it in court. If they plead innocent, it's going to be her word against theirs. She'll make a terrific witness though. We have a little evidence. There are the photographs of her, the blood on her clothes. We found one of her shoes on the roof. We have those people in the Bronx who called the cops after they saw a woman struggling on the roof and our records show a radio run at the time. So far those guys deny they took her out to Connie's sister's home in Jamaica but Brenda could describe that kitchen door. It's not much but it's more than in most rape cases. The woman in Queens is no good, she won't testify against her brother. Sally Clark can claim to be ignorant of anything; she left the apartment before the trouble began. There's no way to know how a jury will react, whether this is enough proof."

The capture of rapists like Stubbs and Connie was an example of skillful, hard work by policemen. But rape is a crime with special qualities and problems. For example, safe and loft detectives, men who work burglary and robbery can become aware of people plotting a caper. The suspects can be put under surveillance and seized midway through the job. On the other hand, there is a well-to-do businessman who has come to the attention of the district attorney's office and the police. He has a habit of using force upon women who are in the predicament of being dependant upon him for jobs or sales. These victims have been unwilling to make a formal complaint; word only got to the law through their private laments to friends.

"We thought of wiring a policewoman and sending her in to see this guy," said an assistant D.A. "But when the defense lawyer gets her on the stand he asks questions like, 'What is your name? But you gave a different name to Mr. X? You asked him for a job, but you really didn't want a job; you already had one?' Her credibility becomes suspect. In addition, you couldn't wait until the guy actually raped her, you just couldn't do that to a policewoman and so it would be tough to bust in just at the right moment, catch him at attempted rape instead of the act itself.

"We also considered staking out his place, waiting until some woman comes out the door, weeping, disheveled, and get her to make an immediate complaint. But can you imagine what would be said if it came out that four cops were hanging around outside waiting while the guy raped a woman?"

Whether Mr. X ever gets caught depends upon a break, a fortuitous chain of circumstances for which the cops can only prepare the ground and then wait.

During a three-month period in 1972, a six foot, young black man raped and plundered until the police in the area "were going bananas," in the words of the assistant D.A. who eventually handled the case. The ravisher—call him Al Bounty—had that rare capacity to put his previous career to work for his benefit. Bounty had been an employee of a firm that delivered packages and messages and his tactics derived from this experience. After noting names on mailboxes, he would ring the doorbell for an appropriate apartment or even use the lobby intercom. When a woman answered, Bounty would say, "I have a package for you." Even though the females he approached had neither ordered anything from a store nor were expecting any gifts, a great many of them could not pass up the possibility of some windfall treat (a number of women did deny him admission and even telephoned the company he claimed to represent to inquire about what was supposed to be delivered).

Face to face with the recipient of his gift, Bounty showed a manila envelope that purportedly contained the delivery slip. His first question was an innocent, "Is your husband or somebody at home who could help me? It's a large heavy thing and I have it in my truck downstairs." The answer supplied Bounty with information on whether any male might interfere with his attack. If there were no men around, Bounty manfully replied, "Perhaps I can handle it myself, but I got to see whether it will fit through your door. Do you have a tape measure handy?"

If she produced one, Bounty would then start to measure the doorway, which of course required that any chain latch be unhooked. And if the woman did not have a tape, Bounty would somehow find one in his pocket.

Once he achieved entrance, Bounty whipped out a knife, blindfolded and gagged the woman, then tied her legs while he ransacked the place for any valuables. Business completed, he untied the legs and pursued his pleasure. The cops had received at least ten complaints of a rapist who used this MO (*modus operandi*).

During one sortie, Bounty came upon a young woman in a nearly empty apartment. The pickings were lean and he was in a surly mood as he focused his attention upon the woman. Then the lobby buzzer rang. "Who's that?" asked Bounty, flourishing a large knife. She had already indicated that she was alone and obviously Bounty was much annoyed with her. A friend was due to help her fix up the apartment but that might only send the rapist into a homicidal rage. Thinking swiftly, the captive said, "It's the moving men, with my furniture," and pointed to the barren rooms. The ploy worked; Bounty fled.

On another adventure, when Bounty untied his victim's legs she flailed at him and he responded with the knife. From the stab wound erupted a large amount of blood, scaring him off. It was actually a superficial puncture and the woman recovered quickly. A day later, however, two uniformed patrolmen, scanning flyers that described Bounty's MO and carried a police artist's composite picture, saw a young black in the neighborhood who matched the general specifications. He even had a manila envelope in his hand.

When accosted, John Martin said he was just a messenger. That clinched it for the cops: They hauled him to the precinct house where the injured woman fingered him. Two other victims, however, could not pick him out of a lineup.

A pair of detectives interrogated Martin. When finished, one of them said, "This is just not a rapist." The local precinct commander regarded the detectives' doubts as the parochialism of the trade. They were sore because patrolmen had made the collar. John Martin was packed off to the Rikers Island penitentiary after he failed to raise the $1500 bail.

Meanwhile, Bounty continued to ply his trade. He went through his routine with another woman. She, however, refused to admit a strange black bearing gifts and told him to leave. She had also received one of those flyers about the delivery-man rapist from the local block association. When Bounty went out the front door of the building, the woman watched him from her window. She telephoned a complete description of him and his clothing to the stationhouse. Within ten minutes, a patrol car spotted Bounty on the street and pulled him in.

In a lineup, Bounty was identified by five of the victims, including the woman who had been stabbed and had originally picked out the innocent Martin. To prevent any attempt by defense lawyers to question the identification procedures, the cops deliberately inserted Martin in the lineups with Bounty. The detectives cut through some bureaucratic underbrush to secure a quick release for Martin. Incidentally, when Bounty used his knife on the woman, she had screamed and a neighbor had heard the commotion. But he had been drying his hair, and in the tradition of the big city was unwilling to risk a damp coiffure in the interests of a screeching next-door tenant. Bounty adamantly pleaded innocent in spite of the evidence. His trial was to be held in the late spring of 1974.

Bounty ran aground because he had fallen into a rut; the routine became so fixed that the cops and private citizens were on the alert for a certain kind of behavior. Rapists also seem to get caught because they so frequently appear to have been in trouble with the cops on other matters and fingerprints and photos are on file.

On a hot summer Sunday, two white women spent the afternoon at a neighborhood swimming pool. As the late afternoon cool lapped at the city, the pair put on their long robes and walked the few blocks to their apartment house. Somewhere along the way, perhaps even at the pool, they had unknowingly attracted the attention of a pair of young black scavengers. At the door of their building, still unaware of the predators behind, one woman produced the key to the outer entrance, opened it and it locked shut behind them.

Unfortunately, while the temporarily frustrated hustlers lounged outside, an old woman rang the buzzer apparatus that unlocked the outer door to permit her keyless daughter to enter, also admitting the two men. They moved swiftly up the stairs, tracking one woman, who, after pausing at her own place, was now on her way to review the afternoon with her friend. When she reached the upper apartment she was allowed in, but failed to snap the lock behind her.

The door now swung open and the male resident, an invalid husband, could do nothing to secure the fortress. "Don't scream," said one of the intruders. "We just want money." He marched the wife into the kitchen and pulled a carving knife from a drawer. The armed man ordered the visiting woman into the bedroom, forced her down onto the bed and raped her. When he had finished, his partner wheeled the invalid into the bedroom and in front of the horrified witness also ravished the woman on the bed.

Taking with them $200 in cash, a watch and a ring, the rapists fled. They were no sooner out of the apartment than the victim, Mabel O'Hara, began to scream. The noise resulted in a call to 911, New York City's emergency assistance number, and subsequently brought a patrol car. The police rushed the assaulted woman to Montefiore Hospital in the Bronx and the Bronx Sex Crimes Squad received notification of the crime. At Montefiore, Mabel O'Hara went through the necessary but humiliating survey of her private parts, the collection of semen, the careful scrutiny for marks or detritus from the offender, such as pubic hair or blood.

It was an hour before Mabel O'Hara returned from Montefiore and Detective John Taldone of the Sex Crimes Analysis Unit, a cop with 20 years on the force, began his interrogation. "She gave us an excellent description of the perpetrators," said Taldone, "and that went out over the police teletype. We also interviewed the other witnesses, the husband, the other woman and the old lady who had seen the two men when they came in the front door.

"The teletype didn't produce any results," said Taldone, "but we brought Mabel O'Hara down to view mug shots. She picked out one guy and said he looked something like one of them, but not exactly. Then we ran through all the guys with similar MOs, guys who followed old women home and grabbed them in the hallway. There was one pair who had been arrested for robbery in the neighborhood previously and had mugged an old Jewish lady in a foyer. I contacted the officer who had arrested the guys. He told me that the two beat the shit out of this woman and she was too frightened to go to court.

"We took Mabel O'Hara to look at pictures of these two, one of them had kind of reddish hair, which was part of the description that she had given us. She was hazy on whether the photographs were the same two guys but they were due to answer another charge of robbery in court in a week.

"We brought Mabel O'Hara to the court, thought maybe she'd pick them out in the crowd. It's the best kind of identification, more impressive than making somebody in a lineup. We waited from nine-thirty in the morning until twelve-forty-five but they hadn't shown. I notified the D.A. and he agreed to call the case. Their names were called but they didn't appear. A lot of times these fellows never make the trial. We're in the hallway of the courthouse saying good-bye, when one of the guys pops out of the elevator. Still Mabel O'Hara wasn't sure that it really was him.

"Anyway, I took him downstairs to central booking;

arrested him and advised him of his rights and then interrogated him. He made a full admission and identified perpetrator number two. We're still looking for him."

Taldone also worked on a case that terrified most of the Bronx. "There were three of them. Their MO was to go down the fire escape between eleven P.M. and six A.M. and break into the houses. They would shine their flashlights on the husband and wife when they found them sleeping there. Using a knife to keep everyone in line, they tied up the husbands, then raped and sodomized the women in front of the husbands. They also took whatever cash or jewelry they could find. Between December of 1972 and March of 1973, they struck eighteen times that we know of.

"These guys all wore navy watch caps, like ski masks, and outside of the fact that they were black we didn't know what they looked like. One woman resisted, pulled off a mask but she still had only a vague idea of what he looked like.

"We weren't getting anywhere until in one of the apartments they made a terrific mess tearing the place apart. We found a piece of a page torn out of a phone book with two telephone numbers written on it. They were from gypsy cabs. Tracing one of these numbers, we found the driver who had picked the three of them up. He had hauled them to a housing project, with four six-story buildings. We went from apartment to apartment, conned people into talking to us. All we had was a composite drawing done from what the girl who pulled away the mask had said. The man we wanted had a big Afro and a long beard. Finally, halfway through the fourth building, somebody thought it might be a fellow in one of the apartments there.

"In his place we found the masks, the navy watch caps with the eyes cut out and some of the stolen stuff. He made full admission and told us where to find the second guy. He gave us the third man.

"We had enough for the burglary, the breaking and entering, but we wanted to make sure these were the guys who had raped the women, and clear the cases. But the victims couldn't identify these perpetrators. They never saw their faces. We ran a reverse lineup. We took three of the couples and we asked the perpetrators to match up husbands and wives. They did it perfectly. It was the bad guys identifying the good guys for a change."

The triumvirate of rapists pled guilty to first-degree armed robbery, and received sentences of 20 to 25 years. Later the case became a matter of contention when a former police lieutenant, Congressman Mario Biaggi, cited it as one more hideous example of plea bargaining. Some feminists protested that it was a typical example of how rapists were able to beat the real rap, the one that would lock them up for a longer period of time.

Actually, the difference was between sentences of 20 to 25 years on the guilty plea and a 30-year sentence if convicted of rape. The prisoners resisted any guilty plea on the rape charges and, conceivably, might have been able to beat the charges because of the corroboration requirement of the New York State law on rape (then in effect). And the victims would all have been forced to undergo the dehumanizing experience of a rape trial. Taldone himself thought the arrangement was adequate. "There's not that much difference in the sentences and you didn't have to put the witness to the trouble or spend the money on a trial. Most of these guys, if really hung-up, will take a plea, even when it doesn't make a big difference in the sentence. Nobody pleads guilty to rape. It's a tough rap to take to prison. Sex criminals are at the bottom of the ladder in prison, especially if they went after kids. The inmates think: This fucking bum might rape my wife or go after my kids.

"Because of the major offense bureau, which works on a federal grant, we can process a rape quickly. I took the invalid husband, his wife and the victim to the district attorney and by one P.M. the next day the case was presented to a Bronx grand jury. Both men were indicted for rape, robbery, burglary, assault with a deadly weapon. They may cop a plea when the trials come up in about three months.

"When I talk to a victim," said Taldone, "I try to make a woman feel at ease. I tell her that I'm a family man myself, a husband and father with four kids. This kind of crime hits me hard. When it's time to go into the actual details, I say I'm not out to embarrass her. I tell her that although it may be painful, these details are important in relation to the legal aspect of the case. I speak to them alone; it's harder to get into intimate details if a third person is around. Maybe take her to a corner of the room so she doesn't feel alone but still we have some privacy.

"I use as nice phrasing as I can but sometimes with illiterate people you have to get down to their fucking level and talk street talk. With black women, they're so used to sodomy, oral and anal, front or back, it's no big deal to talk about it.

"You get some phoney claims. There was a woman on welfare who said she'd been raped but she only wanted an excuse to relocate in a different apartment.

"The perpetrators come in all ages, all sizes, from thirteen years up. Some are family men, some are not, some are ugly, some are handsome. Where we are, it's black on black, black on white, white on white and Hispanic mixed in. I haven't had any cases of white on black, but that's only personal experience; others may have run across that too.

"You rarely catch a guy fleeing from the act. Most cases are broken by investigation, know-how. You find the perpetrator through a case where a similar thing happened. It's partly luck. We knew one guy was hitting the South Bronx certain days of the week. We had a good description of him but that didn't help. We mapped out his MO. He always hit on Thursday or Friday. We figured those must be his days off. Then there was the fact that he always found the woman alone, that it would be two weeks between assaults. We finally figured out that he knew all about his victims, that the reason for the two week intervals was that he was studying his victims, trying to figure out when they were alone.

"Finally he attacked a girl who went to her mother. She didn't even want to come out of the house but a detective finally got her to look at some pictures. She positively identified him from a shot and when we put him in a lineup she positively identified him. Now we

had a whole bunch of people we could call on as witnesses against him. He was actually bashful about telling us how he liked to go down on women."

Taldone insisted that he never had a victim refuse
to talk to him; it's a matter of pride with a detective to
be able to handle those cases assigned to him without
having to call upon some other unit for help. But
aware that victims often complained of insensitive or
even maltreatment by male detectives and recognizing
that many women find it difficult to converse with a
male cop about a crime as intimate as rape, the New
York City police, late in 1972, organized a special unit
to deal with sex crimes. Staffed largely with women,
the Sex Crimes Analysis Unit, sometimes known as the
Rape Squad, perform two major functions. Female
detectives are available to interview any reluctant
women, even going so far as to telephone known victims to urge them to come in for a chat. When a bunch
of teen-agers gang raped an adolescent, members of
the Rape Squad did the major part of the interviewing
and secured enough information so that some of the
youths involved could be arrested. As more and more
policewomen have gone to work in the borough sex
crimes units, the need for interrogations by members
of the Rape Squad has fallen.

A veteran of the Rape Squad is detective third grade
Sylvia Smith. On the force for 15 years, Detective
Smith, a black, had worked the traditional policewoman's roles: juvenile officer, pickpocket unit, matron
duty. But as the crunch of urban crime forced New

York and other cities to stop squandering human resources, she was shifted into undercover narcotics work, perhaps the most dangerous kind of assignment for an officer. After several years of this experience, Sylvia Smith was transferred to sex crimes.

"There is no such thing as a typical rape," said Detective Smith. "Each one is unique. I had a woman here who was absolutely hysterical after she was raped. She was from out of town, hailed a taxi to take her to the bus terminal and the driver took her to a desolate place and raped her, then sodomized her. Then he drove her back, left her off at the terminal.

"The men who got the case called and said, please send a woman to interview her. We can't get anything. Even when I saw her she could barely tell me anything more than the barest facts. I recommended she go to the hospital, she was in such bad shape. Maybe after she calms down we can learn something. Other times the individual remains in absolute control of herself, aware of the smallest details in the experience.

"At first, I usually just let the victim talk. It seems as like it's necessary for them to get it out. The problem is that many times the woman has already told her story twice, to the patrolman she saw first, then maybe to a detective at a precinct station. The woman says, 'Gee, why do I have to keep telling this story.' The problem is that if a person winds up telling the story about an unpleasant experience a number of times, she is going to start leaving out details, details that may be important. The witness starts to decide for herself what's important.

"When you get to the really unpleasant part of their

story they may need a little coaxing. I explain to them why I want to know, not because I want to hear a dirty story but [because] the *way* the man acts is often a very important clue. What he says may be significant. For instance there was one man who would always say, 'I just have to do this, I'm sorry.' When a line like that is used with several women, maybe we can, through similar reports, figure out the area he comes from, or if we pick up a suspect, he can be tied to other cases, perhaps ones that will be even stronger in court.

"We had a complaint about a man who promised girls jobs in show business. He operated in Brooklyn and he would arrange to meet the girls someplace and then would rape them. He had an Afro, but he spoke English with a kind of strange accent. We had him pegged as a West Indian, but when they caught up with him, it turned out he was a Haitian. He was indicted but he skipped after putting up bail.

"Then we started to hear about a man in Manhattan who spoke English with an accent and set up victims with claims that he would get them into show business. However, he didn't have an Afro, but more like a Fu Manchu arrangement. Still, the girls picked him out from the photographs. That's one value in having a unit that is involved with all rape cases. Every single one must be reported to us. We keep track of things."

But knowing who the offender is does not necessarily end the chase. The police, after six months, still had not found the show-biz rapist.

On a filing cabinet at the Rape Squad offices stood a chart labeled "Lipstick Lover." It listed a number of details about crimes that were attributed to a man who picked up the designation of Lipstick Lover because of his MO.

Having hauled his victim off to a place where he felt no fear of discovery, the Lipstick Lover would invariably whip out a tube of what was later determined to be lipstick gloss and then force the woman to commit fellatio. The chart noted each victim's physical description and the one she supplied for the attacker. It also included the location of the assault, weapon used, kind of sex crime committed and other fragments of the pattern.

A police artist sketched a composite of the Lipstick Lover from several descriptions. But with at least ten rapes definitely attributed to him, he continued to avoid apprehension. However, while eating in a diner, an astonished victim suddenly saw the Lipstick Lover come in for a cup of coffee. She suppressed her immediate terror and when he left she rushed to the window and jotted down the license-plate number of his car. Even then, however, recognizing him was not simple. He had taken to wearing wigs in his raiding moments, trimmed his sideburns to hard-hat short. Still, he bore a remarkable resemblance to the artist's rendering. If there's a moral to the rape game, it is attack enough women and sooner or later one will see you on the street and call the cops. At the time this book was completed, the Lipstick Lover was free on bail, awaiting his trial, possibly seeking a good plea bargain.

Perhaps even more important than the interrogation of witnesses, the Sex Crimes Analysis Unit compiles statistics and data on rape. Generally recognized as one of the most underreported offenses, there is also a paucity of information, in rape cases, about who does what to whom and under what circumstances. Without such information, the penal code lacks a foundation composed of the actualities of rape, and, therefore, the police operate without adequate methodology and the public confuses the true threat of rapists with bogey men.

Based upon her experience, Sylvia Smith echoed the beliefs of the members of the Bronx Sex Crimes Squad. "Minorities are the ones most often victimized."

"When a rape case is to go to trial," said John Taldone, "you're much better off if you have physical evidence instead of just eyewitnesses. Sometimes defense lawyers can shake belief in an eyewitness, and juries don't seem to take the word of cops anymore." The fragility of eyewitness identification, including that made by the victim, was never more apparent than in several series of "wrong man" rape arrests that have occurred in recent years. In one instance, it was a detective who became convinced that an innocent man had been trapped and the police officer found the real rapist. In another case, the father of the man in jail spotted a look-alike on a subway platform and parental persistence led to the freedom of a son.

Since rape is an offense that not only raises the question of whether a particular individual committed the act but also of whether indeed a crime *was* committed, statutory and/or case law throughout the United States often make extra demands for supportive evidence. This requirement—usually called corroboration—has come under heavy fire from feminists and some prosecutors who believe it reflects a male self-protective viewpoint. But regardless of the complications of this controversy (which will be discussed later) juries tend to be strongly influenced by presentation of physical evidence. And an important source for this kind of material is the crime lab.

To prove rape, it must first be established that the male penetrated the female. An eyewitness, one in addition to the victim, that is, may testify to the occurrence of sexual intercourse. Equally valid is the statement of the attending physician. A recently ruptured hymen is incontrovertible. In the case of Brenda Adams, the doctor at Lincoln Hospital swabbed out some semen from her vaginal pool. That of course only proved penetration; it is not for the physician to determine whether forcible rape brought about the specimen. A rapist who wore condoms would eliminate some vital evidence against him, provided he was thoughtful enough to tote away the incriminating material.

While the hospital physician draws off what he discerns as semen from an alleged rape victim, courts demand something more than observations with a physican's naked eye. Reports from a crime lab are accepted as conclusive. In the case of a living victim, such as Brenda Adams, slides with samples drawn from the vaginal pool fluids go to the police laboratory. If the woman died, the work is done in the offices of the medical examiner. The standard procedure mixes the suspected semen with a reagent, a chemical that produces a specific reaction—usually a dye color. The technicians are looking for the presence—or absence—of acid phosphotase, a body chemical found in semen. The acid phosphotase test only indicates the possibility that the specimen is the male's life-bearing discharge.

The final examination involves a microscope. Through the lenses, the distinctive shapes of sperm, both live and dead, become visible. Even when the sperm breaks down and dies, its perculiarly shaped head remains. The condition of the sperm, motile or inactive provides confirmation or contradiction of the timetable supplied by the chief witness. Sperm lives in the vagina for up to 48 hours. A victim who concocts a rape charge one afternoon and carries the tale to the cops a few days later, will be confounded if the lab report shows the evidence in her vagina is more than two-days old. "A girl came to us," said Taldone, "claimed she was raped a few hours earlier. But the lab report showed she was negative. What she wanted was a penicillin shot—she was afraid her boy-friend gave her a dose."

At the crime lab, the technicians scrutinized the clothes of Brenda Adams carefully, searching for traces of spermatozoa or blood. "We've recovered stuff a year or two later," says Detective Joseph Iannella, whose police work now consists of peering through microscopes and studying physical evidence obtained at crime sites. "When a crime is committed, whether it's rape or anything else, we send out a forensic team. They examine the premises and bring back anything that might be stained, any fabrics or traces that might lead to the perpetrators. They examine the bed, rug, sofa, back seat of a car. Semen is a white starchy substance. It shows up plain on a dark garment or as an outline on something white [as any boy has noticed after wet dreams] on multicolored fabrics it's hardest to discern.

"I've seen them come back with a chunk of concrete which we examined for the blood on it. When you have something like that you have to get a large enough piece of the stuff for a control, to make sure the chemical reactions we're getting is due to the foreign substance and not something in the concrete, the pillow or the piece of wood itself. It's not always necessary to bring in an item, although we prefer it for the control purposes. Sometimes it's enough to just take a scraping."

Semen does more than simply announce a male's sexual climax. Just as with blood, it is possible to determine, from microscopic examination, the cellular type of the producer. That has played no small part in investigations. In a classic case, a woman was found dead in bed. Autopsy showed that she had been strangled and criminally assaulted. Stained smears of the vaginal contents showed intact spermatozoa. Her pubic hair was matted together with semen, and a seminal stain was found on her thighs. All specimens were interpreted as coming from a Group A man.

On the strength of these results, two suspects, one from Group O and the other a Group B won their freedom. The dead woman's husband, a recent escapee from a state hospital for mental disease became the prime suspect. When seized, however, it was discovered that he held an Immigration Identification Card that labeled him as in Group O. It appeared to clear him, until a routine hospital check discovered the immigration card to be in error. He was Group A and guilty.

In another instance, a young woman came home from a date and shortly afterward reported that she had been raped. Some policemen doubted her account, suspecting that the cry of rape had been raised to cover consensual sex with her boy-friend. Using stains on her panties, tests were made to determine the blood group of the man who had allegedly assaulted her. To the surprise of the cops, the result was Type B. Both the young woman and her boy-friend tested out as Group O.

Oral sodomy—because of the nature of the act—presents a further obstacle to corroboration. The woman may swallow the semen or spit it upon the ground, leaving little opportunity for recovery of a sample. If the victim sees a physician promptly, traces may be still discovered in her mouth. Supportive evidence may consist of stains on her collar or upper clothing or on upholstery if she expectorated on a couch or car seat. One obliging attacker handed his victim a napkin upon completion of the act. His lapse into "kindness" provided damning evidence against him. She kept the napkin and its contents, and turned them over to the cops.

Study of semen to determine cellular type lacks total infallibility, however. About 80 percent of the population are classified by medicine as "secretors." For the other one-fifth, bodily fluids other than blood do not reveal the nonsecretors' cellular type. Furthermore, cellular or blood typing is, at most, proof of innocence or possibility of guilt. It does not positively identify any culprit.

Forensic teams, detectives fine-combing the scene and the physicians or medical examiners turn up more evidence than traces of semen. The blood stains on Brenda's clothes proved to match her type and it was assumed that it came from her lip after Stubbs punched her. Had she scratched her assailants, the blood, skin and flesh left embedded beneath her fingernails could have established the cellular composition of her attackers; unfortunately there was nothing there.

The clothes that Brenda wore received an intensive examination. Somewhere on the garments might be found hairs from the rapist's head, beard or even pubic region. The hairs of Caucasians, Asians, Negroes and North American Indians are as distinct from one another as they are from the hairs of animals. The roots of human hairs have an almost electric bulblike shape while those from beasts are basically long and thin. The center of the hair shaft, which might be compared to the lead in a wooden pencil and which is called the *medulla*, is thinner among humans than among animals. The pigment granules that determine hair color are visible through the microscope as sandlike grains, and those of a human are much finer in size and texture than are those of animals.

Experts can detect the differences between *homo*

sapiens and *fauna* with the naked eye, but distinguishing among humans requires microscopic magnification. Caucasian hair shafts maintain a constant diameter; Negroid, kinky hair shafts, fluctuate in diameter as the hair coils. Mongoloid, Asiatic and North American Indian hair shafts appear similar to the structure of the Caucasian. In Negroid hair, the medium to coarse pigmentation comes in clumps with white spaces in between. An even distribution of pigment granules marks Caucasian and Mongoloid coloring, although the latter is usually not quite as even as the former.

The basic structural hair characteristics do not vary because of where they sprout on a human. But there are, nevertheless, differences to be found between the hair on the head, the limbs and the pubic region. When the Warren Commission attempted to determine whether Lee Harvey Oswald had used a certain blanket, an expert from the FBI testified that examination of hairs taken from the blanket matched the particular quality of Oswald's pubic hairs (plucked from his corpse). Oswald's pubic hairs, reported the expert, were tougher than ordinary; the tips did not round off, as is customary, from constant friction with clothing. The hairs were smoother than usual, lacking a nobbiness ordinarily seen, and there were other distinctive qualities.

Ordinarily, such a matching cannot be accepted as definitive. Like blood, semen and skin, hair characteristics can only indicate that an individual *might* be involved or, conversely, they can exonerate him completely. Still, such evidence when applied in conjunction with other testimony can be very convincing. A 17-year-old Boston boy, Alphonso Pinkney, won the dubious distinction of being among the youngest ever sentenced to the electric chair in 1972. Cited as key evidence was the testimony that Caucasian hairs were discovered on the underwear of Pinkney, a black, and Negroid hairs were located upon the clothing of Miss Marguerite Walters, a raped white woman, who was also beaten and strangled. Incidentally, under Massachusetts law, when murder occurs in connection with a rape, the jury is not allowed to recommend clemency.

Because of changing mores, however, examination of hair is losing some of its currency as evidence. "Intermarriage among races," said Detective Iannella, "makes it increasingly difficult to separate the identity of hairs."

The other main preoccupation of crime laboratories is fibers, snippets and gobbets of garments and furnishings that may confirm the presence of an individual at a felony scene, a robbery, assault, murder or rape. According to Detective Iannella, there are better than 300 different kinds of materials, ranging from the limited natural fibers through the ever-increasing synthetics (progress in new synthetics brings no joy to forensic workers). Under a microscope, a cotton fiber appears as a flattened soda straw that is then twisted, an effect that also can be duplicated at soda fountains. Woolen fibers, drawn as they are from an animal, are easily identified by the scientists who study textiles. Wool falls in the category of hair and they can recognize the characteristics of animal hair, even without magnification. Viscose fibers, one type of synthetic, are composed of chemicals and are very rough around the outside area, having many striations running through them. Regardless of whether the textile is a natural one, or is composed of petroleum by-products, coal tar or a wood derivation, the variations of color plus the twists, the thickness and weavings make for near-infinite variety. The color range in a cotton thread can move through seven or eight shades of green, although to the naked eye one shade would seem identical.

Technicians like Detective Iannella find the textile investigations the most tedious and frustrating. Again, the findings only add to the supportive evidence; they really serve—in the absence of other sources—to hammer shut the case or to mark a trail.

Because of peculiarities in the statutory requirements for the proving of rape and other sex crimes, and because of the highly emotional atmosphere that envelopes trials for sex offenses, collection of all of this kind of physical evidence is even more necessary than in other instances of criminality. Unfortunately, the immediate reaction of many women upon suffering an attack is to bathe and douche their bodies, launder or dump the clothing worn at the time of the crime. As a result, key evidence literally goes down the drain or up an incinerator chimney.

At most, crime-lab findings can only be supportive. Resolution of a rape complaint depends primarily upon the working street cop, the investigating detective, who brings to the work his own peculiar combination of intelligence and experience. "After you've been in this kind of work for a long time," summed up

John Taldone, "you get kind of a gut feeling about things. This girl is lying or this one is telling the truth. Breaking a case takes know-how, putting together everything, tying it up with people who have records and having some luck."

Even then, the "game," if one may classify the contest between cops and rapists as such, is only half won. Before the rapist can be taken off the streets a number of rules must be observed. These rules seem to favor the rapists. To understand why, one has to examine the law as it used to be, and the law as it is now.

III

Origins of Rape Law

Taking a woman by force has been a taboo in all organized societies. The ancient Egyptians dealt with rapists "by removal of the offending parts." Among the early Hebrews, a rapist was put to death if his victim was married. If she was a spinster, however, the offender could pay 50 shekels to the father and then be forced to marry the woman without the possibility of ever obtaining a divorce. The Athenians, too, permitted the ravisher of a maiden to marry her (the custom seems to have been retained in some parts of the world, such as Sicily, where suitors have abducted and raped girls in an attempt to force consent to a marriage upon the parents).

Such authorities as *Stephens Commentaries on the Laws on England* begin their discussions of the legal background for rape laws with the Saxons who ruled the land toward the end of the Middle Ages. The crime was a capital one, punishable by death. When William the Conqueror arrived in 1066, he lowered the penalty to castration and the loss of one's eyes. The Normans seemed aware that even this more modest revenge by the state was subject to possible abuse. As a safeguard against "malicious accusation," says Stephens, a woman was compelled to go to the next town immediately and "make discovery to credible people of the injury."

Having put some credible citizen on notice, the offended women then was allowed 40 days to inform the "High Constable of the Hundred," the coroners and the sheriff of the outrage. Upon being brought to trial and convicted, the accused could escape punishment if the woman accepted him as a husband. Such a marriage also required his consent, but it was an offer not likely to be refused; the alternative was that his eyes would be gouged out, his testicles cut away.

For rape, as for a number of other crimes, the law provided a loophole. Until 1576, assault upon a woman fell into the category of "clergyable" crimes. Punishment, under this provision, was remitted if the rapist took religious orders, conscientiously studying the writings of the church under supervision.

There survives a brief account of a trial for rape from that era. In 1302, in the Cornish Eyre, (a judicial circuit of the times) one Lord Hugh was accused of carrying off a 13-year-old girl to his manor where he allegedly ravished her against her will. The action against Lord Hugh was brought in the name of the king, rather than that of the girl, a significant point in the law of the period because actions brought in the name of the king cost the accused the right to defense counsel. Only in civil matters could someone plead for the accused. Having lost his effort to secure a mouthpiece, Lord Hugh called for dismissal of the king's suit, pleading a clergyable offense, that he was a member of a religious order and subject to the ecclesiastical court for this offense.

The justiciar, the presiding authority for the proceedings, rebutted that defense since Lord Hugh had married a widow, and thus had obviously disqualified himself as eligible to claim membership in a religious order. Nay, nay, answered Lord Hugh and asserted he was fully prepared to prove to the court that his wife had been at the time of his marriage, although a widow, a virgin.

The justiciar refused to accept Lord Hugh's credentials for clergyability, however. The nobleman then huffily announced he'd refuse to participate in any trial before "The Twelve," the number that had already become a requirement for juries. A precursor of John Sirica, the justiciar offered an alternative. Barley bread with no liquid one day, water the next, and then more barley bread without water in a sequence of indefinite length. Lord Hugh saw the rightness of the justiciar's argument; he agreed to accept the verdict of The Twelve. However, he demanded a true jury of his peers, men of his own station in life. This, the justiciar granted.

The process then began. The justiciar requested that the accused read the "challenges" against him. Lord Hugh had to confess that he had never learned the arts of literacy, no small embarrassment since only moments before, when pleading a clergyable offense, he had insisted that he was actively studying the writings of the church. All, however, turned out happily for the "good" Lord Hugh. His peers acquitted him, finding that the rape had been committed by his men, not he.

Sir William Blackstone (the 18th-Century Oxford teacher who rendered the great service of taking the complications of the Common Law and rendering them into something simple that could be understood, if not necessarily by logic then at least on the undeniable grounds of their conformity to the natural law and laws of God), codified the handling of rape charges, among other felonies. Blackstone, while noting that the Romans penalized a man for debauching a woman even with her consent, commented, "But our English law does not entertain quite such sublime ideas of the honor of either sex as to laying the blame of a mutual fault upon one of the transgressors only." The crime of rape, concluded Blackstone, must be against woman's will.

Blackstone quoted the 17th-Century Puritan Lord Chief Justice, Sir Matthew Hale. "Rape is an accusation easily made and hard to be proved and harder to be defended by the accused, though never so innocent."

In the handling of the complaint, Blackstone urged close attention to the time factor. "The jury will rarely give credit to a stale complaint." At the same time, he cautioned against rejection of the cry of rape even from women of easy or no virtue. "The law of England does not judge so hardly of offenders as to cut off all opportunity of retreat even from common strumpets. . . . It therefore holds it a felony to force even a concubine or harlot, because the women may have forsaken that unlawful course of life."

With his restrained faith in "the honor of either sex" Blackstone stressed what has become one of the prickliest aspects of the rape syndrome. "And first, the party ravished may give evidence upon oath, and in law is a competent witness. But the credibility of her testimony, and how far forth she is to be believed, must be left to the jury upon the circumstances of fact that concurs in that testimony." As part of the proceedings Blackstone would admit "her fame" or reputation. Once a strumpet perhaps not always a strumpet, but the career was not to be ignored. Furthermore, Blackstone advised that if the woman "concealed injury for a time," her testimony lost some credibility and if she failed to cry out where she might be heard there was strong evidence that the outrage was feigned.

When it came to putting both Common and statutory law into practice the rape experience proved to be as influenced by public opinion as that of any other felonious enterprise. There was, for example, the interposition of divine justice. An English pamphlet, printed in 1642, reports of an occurrence in the previous month. "So it happened on Monday the 14th of this instant November, that a young virgine, daughter of Master Adam Fisher inhabitant of Devonshire within a mile of Totnoyes, upon some particular occasion happened to go to the said Towne where being busied, partly about her occasions and partly in visiting some friends and kinsfolkes, she was belated, so that her friends were importunate to have her stay all night but she replied that her father would be discontented if she should be absent without his leave, the times being so dangerous and so many Cavaliers abroad. . . ." The author was referring to the state of affairs between Oliver Cromwell's Puritan Roundheads and the pleasure pursuing Cavaliers of the court.

About halfway home in the dark, Master Fisher's daughter heard the noise of a horse galloping toward her and became uneasy: ". . . she plucked up a good heart and went forward until she met with this gentleman, Mr. Ralph Ashley, a gentleman which knew her well. . . ."

When questioned on her destination, the virgin replied she was bound for her father's house. Ashley then asked her identity. Upon hearing the name (it was apparently too dark for him to see her face), "he called to mind her beauty and the Devill straight furnished him with a device to obtain his wicked purpose. 'Sweet heart,' quoth he, 'I know thy father well and for his sake I will see thee safe at thy father's house!' " The villain mentioned that he had seen rowdy soldiers in the area.

She accepted the offer and climbed upon the horse. Ashley rode off the familiar track on the excuse that he would avoid the roisterers. When out of hearing of any inhabitants, "he went about to ravish her, taking a grievous oath that no power in heaven or earth could save her from his lust and with that the poore virgine

with pittious shrikes and cries spake these words, 'O
Lord God of Hosts tis in thy power to deliver me, help
Lord or I perish.' "

Ashley dismissed the invocation with curses and
swore her prayers would be in vain, for there was no
power that could redeem her. "The words were no
sooner uttered, but immediately a fearful comet burst
out in the ayre, so that it was as light as at high noone,
this sudden apparition struck him and all the inhabitants into a great feare and the poor virgine was en-
tranced." Ashley was not so dumbstruck that the sky
light distracted him from sight of the maiden upon the
ground and his purpose thereof. "God-Damnation
alive or dead he would enjoy her," concluded the
pamphleteer.

As Mr. Ralph Ashley was about to fall upon her
body, "a streame of fire struck from the comet in the
perfect shape and exact resemblance of a flaming
sword, so that he fell downe, staggering." Shepherds
in the neighborhood supposedly witnessed the vig-
nette by the light of the comet and hurried to the scene
to bear testament. "They heard a man blaspheming
and belching forth many damnable imprecations."
Cavaliers died hard and unregenerate in Puritan lore.
Questioned about his wound, Ashley, ever a one-
dimensional character, related his intention and what
had happened to him, "by the perverseness of that
roundheaded whore." So he died, raving and blaspheming.

"Reader," finished the author, "here is a precedent
for all those that are customary blasphemers and live

after the lusts of their flesh, especially all those Cavaliers which esteem murder and rapine the chief principles of the religion. . . ."

Not so swift nor so certain was the justice of the English courts, however. Among the records preserved on Common Law cases is that of John Motherhill, committed to Horsham Gaol, September 12, 1785, "charged on oath of Catherine Wade, spinster, with having committed a rape on her body between the hours of eleven at night of the 11th, and five of the morning of the 12th of the said month in the churchyard at Brighthelmstone (Suffolk)."

Some six months later, Motherhill went before a grand jury which returned a true bill and at 4:30 on the afternoon of March 21, the accused stood before Mr. Judge Ashurst, 12 jurymen with names such as Holman, King, Wickham. Mr. Mingay and Mr. Erskine served as the prosecution while Mr. Rous and Mr. Fielding acted for the defense.

Erskine followed his introductory remarks with a presentation of the case. He skillfully described the victim as "a young lady of the most delicate texture and engaging person; she was . . . the most capital artist." He allowed that if he wished to portray "innocence, artlessness and simplicity" he would be proud to take her for his model.

The accused was of a lesser class than Miss Wade and in referring to the scene in the graveyard, Erskine scorned, "Now supposing a moment that she had been inclined to vice, was it probable that she would go with a man like the Prisoner at the bar, voluntarily to brave the inclemency of the weather, when there were men to be found, in the first ranks of life, both for personality and fortune that would have been proud of such a conquest?" Again, the prosecutor was less interested in evidence than personality, it was guilt by class and by character.

As the first witness, Miss Elizabeth Hart testified that Miss Wade had dined and visited with her and her mother, Lady Hart, until about 10 P.M. Arrangements were then made to see the young woman home. "Mr. Griffiths, a surgeon who was present, with Miss Wade and herself went in Lady Hart's chariot for that purpose." Because of the layout of the area, the carriage could not actually draw up in front of the apartment where Miss Wade lived but had to stop at the entrance of a pedestrian passageway that led out to the street. Surgeon Griffiths, less a gentleman than many 20th-Century escorts, simply saw the young woman down the steps leading to the passageway, watched her go some yards up the alley and then left. The doctor told the court that he observed Miss Wade open the outer door to the building and presumed she would enter. As a final note he mentioned having seen a man pass but could not say whether or not it was the accused.

The third witness for the prosecution, a servant of the Wade family, Charles Nye, reported that he had gone to Lady Hart's house to conduct Miss Wade home, only to learn that she had already left. Finding her missing he supposed she was staying with another friend. Not discovering her there, he tramped the streets in search of her, coming only upon Mr. Wade, who in turn became extremely agitated over the absence of his child.

Nye spent the night looking for the young woman. Only upon going back to his employer's house did he learn that she was now home and in the landlord's parlor sat a man who had been taken into custody. Nye told the court that he questioned the prisoner and "asked him whether he had been with Miss Wade, and he confessed he had all night in the church-yard." Nye then played detective, scouring the ground amid the tombstones and found a rim from one of Miss Wade's buckles, some panes of glass broken in the church and "the ground looked as if something had been struggling."

On cross-examination, Nye admitted he could give no explanation for use of the word "struggling" except that the dirt appeared loose and he noticed a footprint. Furthermore, "he admitted there were great numbers of loose women at that time at Brighthelmstone; that they frequently walked the streets in the evenings, and were exceedingly well dressed." The defense had begun to construct one possible line of defense, a case of mistaking Miss Wade for a prostitute. Nye's final contribution was to assert that the door to his master's apartment was locked when he came back from his fruitless tour in search of Miss Wade. The landlady and her maid, with a separate entrance to their rooms, were at home at the time.

The prosecution now called its chief witness, Miss Catherine Wade. She began by explaining that after she left the carriage and walked down the passageway, she found the door to her father's rooms barred and she tried several other doors leading to apartments, such as the landlady's, but could gain no admittance.

While she stood with some perplexity outside her own entrance, the prisoner, whom she had noticed in the immediate area, approached her and asked about her predicament.

"He then told her that he came from her papa and that he (the father) was waiting to take a walk with her. She replied, it was no such thing. She was certain that her papa would not stroll at that hour. Instead of going away, he put his hand upon her bosom. She pushed it from her—he told her she was a very pretty girl, and putting his hand around her neck kissed her; never having been served so before, she was too much frightened to speak; from this he proceeded to put his hand up her petticoats, and the more she repulsed him, the more he persevered."

The villain then forced her from the door and along the street. Miss Wade said she saw no passerby but she screamed for help. Motherhill shut off the outcries with a hand over her mouth and then led her to the churchyard among the tombstones. "He . . . flung her down close by the church, then took up her petticoats and forcibly put his parts into her's; he hurt her very much, lay exceedingly heavy upon her breast, and remained upon her one or two hours, he then got up, but in about a quarter of an hour, threw her down again at the church door; hurt her as much as before, and lay nearly as long upon her; she struggled very much, and did all she could to prevent him. Sometime after he took her to a tomb-stone, where he also flung her down and did the same, during which time it rained very hard, and she was exceedingly wet. He then led her towards the Beech [sic]. She asked him if

57

he was going to take her home? To which he answered, yes: All this time it poured of rain, and was very dark. When he came to the steps that led down to the Beech, he looked about as if apprehensive some person was near but perceiving nobody, he forced her down the steps, and frightened her terribly, by swearing very much at her: She asked him, if he was going to drown her? He replied he wished the water was higher. After he had forced her into the machine [the contrivance built along the beach for bathing purposes], he flung her down and did the same as he had done in the church-yard; at which times she felt the emission of something into her body; this he repeated while they remained in the machine. By throwing her down in the machine he hurt her elbows and her thighs, and after he had used her in this manner, he forced her to remain all night with him; she would have got away from him, if possible, but could not before daylight when he led her out of the machine, and followed her towards home; where, when she arrived, she was too much frightened and agitated to relate what had happened to her."

Mr. Rous now cross-examined in an attempt to shake the tale. From the witness he drew the admission that while "she disapproved of the prisoner's conduct while at her father's door, she had no idea of his intentions; yet she admitted on much pressure, that from putting his hands on her bosom and up her petticoats, she was convinced his intentions were something improper. Her not crying out when he forced her along the passageway between occupied houses she attributed to fright." However, the rapist did not take hold of her as she went along the street but permitted her to go first while he followed at some distance. She mentioned no attempts to flee and although lights flickered in the windows they passed, she did not attempt to knock at either doors or windows, something she could have accomplished before Motherhill could have seized her.

Rous referred to the original interrogation of Miss Wade—British jurisprudence was sufficiently advanced so that some record of this examination was retained for use at the actual trial. In her deposition, the woman reported that her assailant had pushed her to the ground immediately upon entering the churchyard and the attack by the church window was his third assault. However, in the trial she now told the court that the incident by the church window was the first attack and Rous demanded an explanation for the inconsistency.

The witness answered that her present story was the accurate one. The scribe for the trial noted, "He [Rous] found several other contradictions . . . one particularly, where she stated to have asked the prisoner, whether he meant to drown her, to which she had made him originally reply, No, and now she made him answer something about the waters being higher; to which he [Rous] could get no other reply than what she now stated was the truth." Presumably, it was a matter for the jury to decide; that time had either clarified or clouded her memory, or that she and the prosecution had embroidered the original complaint.

As a further inconsistency, the defense lawyer pointed out that in the pretrial deposition she had said that he had led her into the bathing contraption not forcibly, but simply by the hand. When light had begun to brighten the beach, she had mentioned going home as women would be arriving to use the area soon. She had said that he then assisted her out of the machine and escorted her home. "In this cross-examination her replies seemed frequently to bear a palpable contradiction to one another, as well as to the deposition she had previously made. . . ."

Father Wade then took the stand to tell the court that his daughter had been educated at the Benedictine Convent at Calais for the previous 12 or 13 years and had been in England only three months before she met with what he called "this distressing misfortune."

Wade recounted how he had spent the night searching for his missing child, only to be advised that she was home, and that a man seen following her home had been taken into custody. He went to see the man and upon asking him whether he had been all night with his child, he answered, "I have been a very wicked wretch, and have deserved to be hanged a long time;" but made no other reply to his question. Upon the accused man's grimy hand Wade observed blood. He demanded of Motherhill its origin.

"It was Nature," answered the prisoner.

Mr. Wade advised the court that a constable eventually arrived and the bloody, filthy shirt worn by Motherhill was stripped from his back to be retained for court evidence.

Landlady Ann Sycamore testified next. As a fellow occupant of the house with the Wades, Mrs. Sycamore said of the victim "there did not breath a more pure and innocent-minded creature, unfortunately, indeed, for her, her understanding was very far from a strong one."

When the accused was brought into the house, Mrs. Sycamore arranged for Miss Wade to see if she knew her abuser and the girl had identified him. At this moment, the prosecution offered in evidence the clothes worn by the victim. "Her shift, petticoats and gown were in such a situation as to strike every person in court with horror; the rest of her clothes were much torn and entirely spoilt." (Not surprising for items that had spent a night exposed to mud and rain and then been stuffed away in a constable's closet for six months.)

Mrs. Sycamore upon undressing and bathing Miss Wade noticed a bruise on her left thigh, marks of fingers in her right shoulder, a bruise upon the small of her back and one on each elbow. The prosecution took the opportunity to clear up one possible question in the mind of the jury about the absence of passersby at the hour in which Miss Wade was accosted. Mrs. Sycamore observed that it was not customary for the streets of Brighthelmstone to be deserted at that hour but the weather for the evening, dark, stormy and disagreeable, might have driven everyone inside.

Surgeon Lowdell, summoned by Wade to examine his child's body, told the court his findings. He confirmed the existence of the bruises and marks observed by Mrs. Sycamore. "As to any violence of another kind having been committed on her body, the parts, though somewhat irritated, had not, he thought, the appearance necessary to warrant him to declare such was the case; for although he found the membrane hymen gone, it was well known to be frequently the case from a thousand circumstances besides coition, and that single circumstance excepted, there was not, in his opinion, any grounds for supposing she ever had any connection with man."

A second physician, Mr. Griffiths, the escort, also examined the body and declared "there was every reason to conclude from the appearance, that she had suffered great violence, and had been violated. When he first saw her the parts were greatly inflamed and he ordered them washed with a sponge, dipped in soap and water; this he did for the double purpose of stopping the inflammation, and preventing, if possible, any infection; although he had very little apprehension, provided the man had been infected with a venereal complaint, of its taking effect; as her body at the time, was, no doubt in a state of natural evacuation." Griffiths insisted that although "the effects of nature, certainly something, had aggravated a more than common overflow—and what could possible act as such an aggravation at that time, as violent and repeated coition."

Surgeon Lowdell disagreed with his colleague. He did not believe that either soap and water five or six hours after the act, or a female in that situation, would be "safe from the infection." He was rather well in advance of the science of venereal disease for the time. Lowdell rather thought that "the vessels of her body would be more open, she would be the more likely to take it."

Prosecutor Erskine considered the question irrelevant to the case but Lowdell remarked that he examined Motherhill and discovered him to have a "gleet," a discharge symptomatic of gonorrhea.

The prosecution rested and the judge asked the prisoner if he wished to speak. "I leave it entirely with my Counsel," answered Motherhill.

Speaking for his client, Fielding declared, "My Lord, the evidence for the Prosecution having proved what we meant to have called witnesses for—that from the number of common women continually about the streets, it was possible to mistake."

Judge Ashurst charged the 12-man jury. The recorder of the trial reported that the magistrate "took an infinite deal of pains to explain the nature, and what constituted the crime of a rape according to the laws of this country."

The jury then began its deliberations. After half an hour they inquired whether they had any alternative between death or acquittal. "His Lordship informed them there was none; and that they must bring in their verdict either Guilty or Not Guilty." After what was calculated as "a few minutes" consultation, the foreman reported that "while they labored under some doubts, they could not do otherwise than pronounce him Not Guilty."

Judging from the last inquiry put to Magistrate Ashurst, the jurymen shrank from a guilty verdict, less from belief in innocence than from a reluctance to levy the extreme penalty. Penologists have often debated whether severe punishments do not become self-defeating as veniremen refuse to take the burden for assessing long prison terms or execution.

Not all 18th-Century Englishmen who sat in judgment of their peers exhibited the same delicacy as those who deliberated the fate of John Motherhill.

The *Newgate Calendar* or *Malefactors' Bloody Register*, a journal of criminal cases of 18th-Century England designed to deter those who might stray from the straight and narrow paths of bawdy Britain, contains a number of horrid examples of the fate dealt out to rapists. The *Newgate Calendar*, like the one done at Tyburn, another prison of the period, was written by chaplains, and the exhortations and descriptions concern themselves as much with matters moral as criminal.

In an introduction to the case of Francis Charteris, whose name was a terror to female innocence, the authors offer a model of 18th-Century enlightenment on the subject of rape. "It [the crime] is certainly of a very heinous nature, and, if tolerated would be subversive of all order and morality; yet it may still be questioned how far it is either useful or politic to punish it with death; and it is worth considering whether, well knowing that it originates in the irregular and inordinate gratification of unruly appetite, the injury to society may not be repaired without destroying the offender."

The accused, Francis Charteris, was the archetype scapegrace. Wealthy, related to the best families in the nobility, he first disgraced himself as a cardsharp and usurer while serving with the British military forces in Brussels.

Court-martialed and cashiered, Charteris then at-

tracted notice with a tale of a fake robbery that resulted in a landlord and a group of church friars raising
a purse of significant magnitude to mollify Charteris.

Back home in Scotland, Charteris bought himself
another commission and rose to a colonel. When he
sat down to play cards with the Duchess of Queens-
bury one evening, Charteris thoughtfully arranged for
a mirror to be placed in a strategic position. Thus
foresighted, he won £3000 from her grace. As a result
her outraged husband forced through a law that limited gaming. While Charteris prospered in such kinds
of investments, he also contrived to hire country girls
as servants, "the consequence of which was, that their
ruin soon followed," said the Newgate authors.

He ran afoul, however, when he pursued a Miss Ann
Bond. She had refused his favors when she entered his
service, even though he allegedly offered a purse of
gold and an annuity for life. Passion inflamed the colonel. While Ann Bond stirred the coals in the colonel's
fireplace one morning, he suddenly seized and committed violence on her, first stopping her mouth with
his nightcap. Afterward, on her avowal that she would
prosecute him, "he beat her with a horsewhip and
called her by the most approbrious name."

Ann Bond went straight to a gentlewoman of her
acquaintance and a grand jury indicted Colonel Charteris. Held for trial at Newgate, he bought off the heavy
chains that encumbered him, secured a private room
in the prison and a man to wait upon him.

When the trial commenced, in the fashion of rape
defenses, "every art was used to traduce the character
of the prosecutrix, with a view to destroy the force of

her evidence . . . but her character was so fair . . . that every artifice failed . . . a verdict of guilty was given against the colonel who received sentence to be executed in the accustomed manner" [hanging].

The judge and jury evidently did not believe in the milder solutions proffered by the chaplains in their opening remarks on the Charteris case. But where reasoned arguments failed, money persuaded. In return for a large sum of money tendered to a Scottish official, plus an annuity settled on Ann Bond, Charteris received a royal pardon.

After his death, a contemporary wit penned an inscription to go with a mezzotint of the colonel standing before the bar with his hands bound:

> Blood! must a colonel, with a lord's estate,
> Be thus obnoxious to be a scoundrel's fate?
> Brought to the bar, and sentenced from the bench,
> Only for ravishing a country wench?

The *Newgate Calendar* also contains a long account of the trial of Frederick Lord Baltimore and two accomplices for the rape of Sarah Woodcock. Baltimore was the son of George Calvert, elevated to a peerage by King James I and recipient of a large tract of Maryland from the king. In pursuit of his classical education, the scion had traveled to the sites of antiquity, including Turkey, where he discovered in the Turkish seraglio a taste that fitted his own. Back home, he had built into his house a series of apartments that conformed to the needs of a harem.

Miss Woodcock, a dry goods clerk, resisted Baltimore who employed a number of strategems that culminated in an abduction. Held a prisoner in the Baltimore mansion she eventually was forced to yield. When she finally made her escape, charges of rape followed. A jury, however, accepted his lordship's explanation of the affair as that of a libertine with a loose woman. Baltimore's defense included the assumption that Miss Woodcock was physically stronger than he. However, the *Newgate Calendar* writers considered Baltimore to be a guilty man whom circumstances had contrived to free. It seems fair to guess that juries of the time found it more difficult to convict a rich man of such a base crime than one lowly born. A humble clerk, Benjamin Russen, in the same time period, went swiftly to the gallows for rape.

The procedures followed in England were exported to America, as exemplified in the trial of Richard D. Croucher, in July of 1800. The indictment: "The Jurors of the people of the State of New York present that Richard D. Croucher, late of the City of New York, in the County of New York, laborer, not having the fear of God before his eyes but being moved and seduced by the instigation of the devil [until we became overwhelmed in the encumberances of corporate law, poetry resided in the breasts of men of legal training], on the 23rd of April. . . . with force of arms upon one Margaret Miller, spinster, in the peace of God . . . violently and feloniously did make an assault on her the said Margaret Miller then and there feloniously did ravish and carnally know her against the

67

form of the statute [lawyer's poetry, however, occasionally must end lumpen]."

Attorney General Cadwallader D. Colden delivered an opening definition of the crime. "He who has carnal knowledge of a woman against her consent is guilty of Rape [sic] even with her consent, and such consent is extracted from her through fear."

Margaret Miller was a 13-year-old girl who had lived for several years with a kind of foster mother, Mrs. Stackhavers. According to Margaret Miller, who required a few moments respite in court to recover from embarrassment "wiping away the tears which ran fast down her cheeks," Richard Croucher sold stockings fairly regularly to Mrs. Stackhavers. In April he asked if the girl might come to his lodgings to clean up the place since he was expecting to use the premises as a kind of showroom for some of his wares.

Mrs. Stackhavers agreed, reluctantly, said Margaret Miller. One evening the girl traveled to the rooms on Greenwich Street where Croucher lived. The arrangement was for her to share a bed with a servant girl, enabling her to get an early-morning start at the chores.

Once in the apartment, however, Croucher locked her in his room, undressed her, then undressed himself. "He used force, he did what he would and hurt me very much, so much that I could hardly get home." She claimed to have made her escape the following dawn, waiting until Croucher fell asleep, "till I could see as to find the door." Later she clarified the matter, advising the court that daylight permitted her to locate the key to the door.

Attorney General Colden inquired, "Did you not cry out?"

"At first I screamed, but he said if I did not hold my tongue, he would put me out of the way. I cried all the time but not loud."

Q. Did you tell Mrs. Stackhavers?

A. No, I was afraid. He used to visit our house every day.

Indeed, the plot thickened when matron Stackhavers and Croucher married a fortnight after the alleged rape. The prosecutor asked how the crime came to light?

A. He told Mrs. Stackhavers about it.

Q. How came he to do it?

A. He got angry with me one day. . . . He told her he had lain with me with my consent." On further questioning Margaret denied ever giving consent.

Apparently, Mrs. Stackhavers believed the tale of her husband at first. Although she and her new spouse quarreled constantly, and he whipped the girl for her "slothfulness," Mrs. Stackhavers advised the teenager to seek a home elsewhere. Margaret Miller seemed well-disposed to a new arrangement, for on at least three occasions Croucher, not content with corporeal punishment, forced her to leave the house and spend the night on the streets.

With Margaret Miller in a new abode, the matter might never have come to the attention of authorities but relations between Croucher and Mrs. Stackhavers degenerated to the point of such ill treatment that the woman went to the police. In detailing the sins of her husband, she referred to his self-confessed adventure with the child and the girl's insistence that she had not ever given consent. Representatives of the police sought out Margaret Miller, with the result that Richard Croucher now stood in the dock.

Mr. Justice Benson, Mayor Richard Varick, recorder Richard Harrison and Alderman Selah Strong, the four judges sitting, took it upon themselves to pin down the witness to discover, "in precise terms, whether she was certain that the prisoner had committed the crime for which he was now on trial." She replied in the affirmative.

Defense attorneys Brockholst Livingston and Washington Norton cross-examined the girl, seeking at first to discover if the alleged rape had really been so traumatic.

> **Q.** Did you miss school next day?
> **A.** I was so lame, I could not go, I lay o'bed.
> **Q.** Has not Mrs. Stackhavers threatened to turn you out of doors, if you did not complain of him?
> **A.** No sir.

On further interrogation, Margaret Miller charged that Croucher, even when living as the husband of Mrs. Stackhavers, propositioned her and she made her escape only by running out of the house.

Abiel Brown, landlady for the newlywed Crouchers appeared for the prosecution. She swore that she had overheard Croucher tell his wife that he was certain the "girl is a whore"; and he was determined to know if it were so, and therefore he had lain with her one night and was satisfied that it was so." (Rather an extended and incriminating "overheard.")

> Q. Did you understand ma'am from what he said that he had a connection with her?
> A. Yes, I did.
> Q. That he had carnally known her?
> A. Yes sir.

Cadwallader Colden rested his case and defense counselor Morton took over. Saying that his client had already been proven innocent by the previous testimony, Morton nevertheless insisted upon putting forth an argument for acquittal. He read passages from law commentaries and Matthew Hale. "I only mention these instances that we may be more cautious upon trials of offenses of this nature, wherein court and jury may with so much ease be imposed upon, without great care and vigilance. The seriousness of the offense many times transporting the judge and jury with so much indignation, that they are hastily carried to the conviction of the person accused thereof by the confident testimony sometimes of malicious and false witness." Defense lawyers in modern rape cases use other words to deliver the same message.

Morton introduced a deposition from grocer George Richer, excused from a court appearance on the grounds of illness. Richer, conceivably a business associate of the accused, said that Croucher often complained of the girl's "sauciness." Richer deposed that about three weeks before the marriage (which would have been one week before the incident at

Croucher's lodgings) he came upon "Croucher and Margaret Miller, who was standing between the legs of Mr. Croucher, resting her hands upon his thighs, as this witness thinks, in an improper way."

Richard Alstine also appeared for the defense. He occupied the room next to Croucher's and told the court that the walls were thin, thin enough for him to hear chairs scraping, but never did he hear any girl cry out or scream in the adjoining apartment. Under cross-examination he confessed that he seldom returned to his room before ten or eleven at night, which meant that he most likely was not present at the critical moments described by Margaret Miller.

Both sides had completed their cases except for final statements. Colden quoted from the commentaries of Hawkins, "Offenses of this nature are no way mitigated by showing that the woman at last consented to the violence, if such consent was forced through fear of death or of duress. Nor is it any excuse that she consented after the fact," a suggestion that the unwanted gift might possibly turn out to be highly valued upon sampling.

For the defense, Livingstone addressed the jury. "No other crime excites greater abhorrence or indignation. . . . When a female who is entitled to our protection is seduced or violated, there is universal dispostion in our sex to avenge the injury." It was an age in which male paternalism excited little resentment. "It is bad if an infant of tender age falls a sacrifice to the arts of a man of the prisoner's appearance [Croucher, guessing from several remarks during the trial, must have been a singularly ugly man]. Whatever

72

misconduct, it has been with her consent. The passion may be as warm in a girl of her years as in one of more advanced years." (Boys a year older, however, were still considered, by law, as being incapable of fulfilling their passions.)

More than 170 years ago, Livingstone whipped out a perennial demon to sway the jury. "Don't think of her youth. Who that is acquainted with the dissolute morals of our own city does not know females, many of them to be found living in a state of open prostitution at the early ages of twelve or thirteen."

Concluded the lawyer, "I suppose he is guilty of having most shamefully seduced and ruined the girl, but the moment that seduction is put on the same footing and confounded with rape, consequences most dreadful are to be apprehended." He created a piteous vision of every courtier who achieves seduction going to the hangman for rape, if Croucher were adjudged guilty.

In rebuttal, Cadwallader Colden scorned any determination to acquit based upon possible mistaken judgments in the past. He explained that it was thought unnecessary to offer any character witness for the young girl. "We have relied upon the natural perception, that a child of her age could not have any wanton desires." Colden dismissed out of hand the notion that the cry of rape was the means for Mrs. Stackhavers to eliminate her odious spouse.

To the recorder fell the duty of making the charge to the jury. "There has been a connection between them and the single question that remains is whether it was against consent."

After only four minutes, the all-male jury returned to declare Richard Croucher guilty of rape. Pronouncing the sentence a day later the recorder said, "In several countries such a crime means ignominious death but through the humanity of the modern code the prisoner will spend life in a state prison." Croucher suddenly spoke out, not to protest the sentence or the trial but to solemnly swear that he had never had "connection with the girl."

The recorder ended the affair, "It is too late to make declarations of this sort."

The odds upon survival for any long period of time in a state penitentiary in 1800 must have been rather low, but at that Croucher was spared a fate handed out to a Connecticut black freeman who went by the name of Anthony. He went to the gallows in 1798 and while the circumstances of the crime and the trial remain obscure, the offense was enough to stimulate clergymen to expound on human villainy.

The peculiarly American brand of John Calvin belched forth: "But so violent and inflammatory are sinful principles in the heart of man so strong and perpetual in the temptation to the commission of crimes against chastity and so deep is the veil of secrecy which the modesty of the most profligate throws around these transactions, that it is impossible always to restrain them, either by the penal law of God or men."

There is some evidence that until the United States became an independent nation, and the more virulent strains of religion erupted in the land, a gentler aspect was turned toward sexual crimes. During colonial times, treason, murder and grand larceny were not bailable offenses (the British had their own value of things) but rape fell among what were considered "minor" crimes and was thus bondable. Rapists could enjoy freedom until trial. By the 19th Century, possibly in the wake of the last great fundamentalist surge, the attitudes on sexual transgressions had hardened, and the written laws began to take a very hard line. As a counterbalance, those requirements intended to preserve the innocent against the terribly severe punishments to be meted out to sinners also appeared.

In Great Britain, Elizabeth (the "Virgin" Queen) appropriately enough had removed rape from the list of clergyable offenses. It was under the acknowledged representative of 19th-Century respectability, Queen Victoria, that the British finally settled the handling of the crime. Permanent codification of the law in 1861 made rape a felony punishable by a maximum of life imprisonment. Complainants need not produce corroborative or supportive evidence for a charge to be brought.

In the United States, however, as early as 1848, according to legal scholar Edith Barnett, New York had introduced the necessity of some buttressing argument for a complaint of sexual misconduct. The constant answer to a problem, "there ought to be a law . . ." for sex crimes rose in the next 125 years to deafening decibels, blocking out good sense as well as justice.

IV

The Law Now

Advised that the Law of England made woman the equal of man, Mr. Bumble of Dickens's *Oliver Twist* retorted, "If the Law says thus and so, then the Law is an ass." Whether it is an ass may be debated, but if it is, you can be sure it's a Jack and not a Jenny.

Start with the 1952 edition of the *Corpus Juris Secundum*, a series of canons that established the basic points of reference for consideration of rape as a crime. It is here that one finds the inglorious description of rape as a form of knowledge. But going on, the *Corpus* sets the boundaries for the definition of rape, however objectionable the terminology.

"Carnal knowledge of an unchaste woman by force and against her will is rape, the mere fact of her unchastity being neither a defense nor mitigation. . . ." While Blackstone considered it necessary to include the common strumpet on grounds that she might have seen the error of her ways, the *Corpus* simply makes the deciding issue the question of consent or lack of it. In the instance of the slut, the cry of rape may be heard because a customer has refused to pay the agreed sum or else has turned unnecessarily rough during the act. The New York Sex Crimes Section noted four prostitutes as rape victims in the the first six months of 1973.

The *Corpus* most clearly accepts the differences between the sexes with its confession, "The crime of rape can be committed by a male person only." The dream of the young man accosted by three women and forced at gunpoint to service all of them has wandered through many male fantasies. Such a tale even made the newspapers in 1945. The ability of the male to perform under such stress is not accepted by the authors of the *Corpus*. Research by students of human sexual behavior, such as associates of Alfred Kinsey, confirm the ineffectiveness of the male when under the gun. So-called homosexual rape, forcible buggery, is covered by statutes on sodomy. The laws of all states thus specifically speak only in terms of the male visiting outrage upon the female, although at one community meeting in Brooklyn, a male attendee constantly interrupted the talk by asking when rape of males would be discussed. He attributed the phenomenon to "Womens' Lib." However, a woman may be accused of a rape if she aids and abets a man, holding the gun for example. The principle parallels that of the lookout in an armed robbery who will also be charged with murder should one of his companions kill anyone during the crime. On this basis alone, a number of women have been accused of rape.

But there are men who have been issued a license to obtain carnal knowledge against the will and without the consent of a specific female. The certificate of permission is called a marriage license. The *Corpus* instructs: "Rape cannot be committed by a husband on his wife, either because such intercourse is not considered unlawful or because by marriage she consents to the intercourse with her husband, which [permission] she cannot withdraw." While a husband may be arrested for simple or atrocious assault upon his wife, if he adds sexual intercourse to his endeavors he risks no added penalty. A spouse who in a gesture of friendship assists another male to rape his wife, however, can legally be held for rape.

The only other exception to this principle of rape involving partners in connubial bliss, is the case of a husband and wife who have separated or are divorced. For example, a few years ago, a young couple in Brooklyn enjoyed the swingers' life—group sex, freely chosen partners, homemade pornographic photographs. She wearied of both the orgies and the husband, and they separated. One day the husband appeared at her office and threatened to flash a set of photos of her from the good old days to her employer and fellow workers if she refused to submit to him. The wife accompanied the husband to his apartment where they engaged in sexual intercourse. As a demonstration of good faith, he permitted her to share his grasp on the incriminating pictures. When the husband had satisfied himself, he didn't relinquish his hold, but, rather, he attempted to pull the photos away as insurance for return engagements. The photographs tore apart in the tug of war and she left to call the cops and charge him with rape. During the presentation to the grand jury, the critical issue of supportive evidence centered upon the fragments of photographs that the woman retained. These were the instruments of duress and it was critical to the case that they be identified. One snapshot was a frontal view of a naked man. During the struggle the head of the man had been torn off. The woman steadfastly insisted that this was a shot of her husband. The D.A. inquired, how she could be so certain when the face was missing? Jurymen, judge and even D.A. held their breaths as the witness cleared her throat to answer. "I recognize the wristwatch he's wearing." Tentative as that might seem, along with other evidence, there was enough to scare the husband into copping a sexual abuse plea.

The certificate of marriage confers upon the husband the right to sexual intercourse against the will or without the consent, but the issue becomes clouded in Common Law marriages. The *Corpus* takes no recognition of the couple that has lived together for years without benefit of ceremony. When she pleads one night, "I've got a headache," and he asserts himself for that which has been regularly granted him over a period of time, he becomes eligible for charges of rape. Conviction by a jury will be difficult in such instances, however.

The *Corpus* calls penetration, however slight, a necessary element in rape. Emission by the male is not required for the finding of rape but, on the other hand, emission without penetration falls short of the definition of rape. During the Giles-Johnson rape case in Maryland during the 1960s, one of the issues concerned a contradiction in the testimony of the prosecutrix as to whether two or three men "raped" her. Under prosecution prodding she asserted in court that she had originally been confused at the preliminary hearings because one of her attackers had not had an emission although he had, she swore, penetrated her.

In the critical matter of lack of consent or against the will, the bible for jurisprudence says, ". . . the law requires something more than mere absence of consent, there must be actual resistance or excuse incompatible with consent for its absense . . . the resistance must be in good faith and not a mere pretense or as stated otherwise, it must be real or genuine and active and not feigned or passive or perfunctory. . . ."

Furthermore, the principle is refined. "The female need not resist as long as either strength, endurance or consciousness continues [lawyers knew better than to demand the dedication of "I'd rather have died than submit"] but rather the resistance must be proportionate to the outrage, allowances must be made for relative strength, the uselessness of continued resistance." In state after state, courts have felt it necessary to reiterate the point. The sovereign state of Nebraska, through its supreme court, stated "Resistance or opposition by mere words is not enough, the resistance must be by acts, and must be reasonably proportionate to the strength and opportunities of the woman. She must resist the consummation of the act, and her resistance must not be a mere pretense, but must be in good faith, and must persist until the offense is committed." In the abstract, the Nebraska top benchers echo the *Corpus* clearly. But court decisions dredged from library research and written in the solitude of a judge's chambers do not equal the decision-making process for a woman faced by a man with a gun, knife or a very heavy fist. Must her resistance in "good faith" persist until he does orthodonture with a fist?

In another case *Gordon* v. *State* (1946), the state of Alabama remarked, "The consent given by the prosecutrix may well have been implied as well as express, and the defendant would be justified in assuming the existence of such consent if the conduct of the prosecutrix toward him at the time of the occurrence was of such a nature as to create in his mind the honest and reasonable belief that she had consented by yielding her will freely to the commission of the act. Any resistance on the woman's part falling short of this measure would be insufficient to overcome the implication of consent."

The language of statutes on rape usually includes the phrasing, "without her consent or against her will." The meaning was clarified by case law both in England and the United States. In Massachusetts in 1870, two gents, Burke and Green, were convicted of having raped Joanna Caton after she had become drunk. In their appeal, Burke and Green attempted to wriggle free on the proposition that they had not gained their carnal knowledge against Joanna Caton's will; she was just too stupefied to be for or against sexual relations. The higher court rejected the petition. The British arrived at the same conclusion under *Regina* (Victoria) v. *Camplin*. The laws covering rape and other sexual crimes specifically include, as protected, a woman who has been drugged, intoxicated, duped or is either mentally retarded or deranged. The principle is linked to the incapacity of the female to consent or to resist. The Brooklyn dentist who sodomized a patient under anesthesia became subject to prosecution under this proviso. In the mid-1960s, a 315-pound pharmacist on the Upper East Side of Manhattan inveigled women to try an oral "fingernail hardener" with the result that they found themselves drugged and raped in a motel a few hours later.

By case law, the deception must involve the actual act of sexual intercourse, not the circumstances surrounding it. In several instances, physicians took advantage of patients. In what might be called a scientific variation of Boccaccio's monk "putting the devil back in hell," an Iowa doctor, shortly before the turn of the 19th Century, informed a 16-year-old girl that she had an upside down uterus and that the only cure was sexual intercourse, with himself naturally at the controls. He was convicted of rape but a higher court overturned the decision on the grounds that she was aware of what he was about to do and was only duped as to the purpose. In another case, however, the medical man went to prison for misrepresenting the treatment itself.

Consent not having been given before the act cannot be conferred postcoitally either. J. Dunbar attacked Bridget Donovan in 1888 and the Massachusetts Supreme Court upheld the conviction, even though Miss Donovan subsequently tried to excuse her assailant. The state contended that in spite of the special interpersonal quality of a sex crime, the matter was the Bay State against Dunbar, not *Donovan v. Dunbar*. The fact that actions against felons are taken in the name of the state rather than the injured party becomes lost to view in many instances. There is a demand for justice for the victim but that is not the concept under which criminal prosecutions operate. The decision against Dunbar was another affirmation of this basic theorem of jurisprudence.

In the United States the laws regarding forms of sexual expression other than heterosexual intercourse are not covered by the rubric of rape. "The commission of sodomy per anum [rectum] or per os [mouth] is not the commission of a rape, although both offenses involve carnal knowledge of the victim . . . sodomy involves abnormal and perverted sexual relations. . . ." explains the *Corpus*. The British, through the Wolfenden Commission's Report in 1967 totally abandoned prosecution of all sexual activities entered into by consenting adults. The English had never been as severe as Americans on forms of sexual expression other than rape (except for male homosexuality, as in Oscar Wilde's case). Fornication and adultery had been treated by ecclesiastical courts, and when these were abolished, following the Reformation, the civil courts did not pursue the behavior. In the United States, however, all sexual behavior has been regulated by law.

In much of the United States the varieties of sodomy —both as to sexes and to orifices—are often barred even to married individuals by law. For the unmarried, the risks of sodomy are greater. In New York, as in some other jurisdictions, it is not legally possible to consent to sodomy. Therefore, all expressions of homosexuality become illegal, even though all parties enter into one another by mutual agreement. In addition, oral to genital, genital to oral contact becomes proscribed.

The British tradition for the processing of rape claims began to crumble in America during the mid-19th Century. Some states, New York included, then began writing into the penal law, demands that the chief witness be supported by additional facts. The initial move in New York centered on those statutes that related to seduction with the promise of marriage or claims of abduction for the purposes of prostitution. By 1886, the New York State Legislature, an all-male body, had rewritten its code in such a fashion as to require corroboration for rape charges. That was not made necessary for other kinds of sexual crimes, such as forced sodomy, until 1967, a sort of highwater mark in loading the female with the onus of proof. (Until that year a man might more easily be charged and convicted of forced sodomy than rape.)

As New York's law stood in 1967, sex offenses required that charges of three essential elements—force or lack of consent, penetration and identity of the perpetrator—be buttressed beyond the mere word of the victim. (The penal law specifically announced that the purpose was to protect the innocent.)

Insistence upon further evidence than the complaint of the woman rests on three assumptions. First among these is that there exists a sufficiently large number of females who will cry rape as a means of revenge or to disguise their own lascivious behavior. The second premise is that the crime itself is so heinous in the eyes of a jury that the mere charge of sexual assault will stampede people into a guilty verdict (one of the points in Croucher's defense). The third belief is that the defendant cannot prove his innocence of forcible rape, particularly if the issue is one in which the sexual congress of the pair has been stipulated and at issue only is consent. All of the assumptions benefit the accused; the accused is always male; it is the male-oriented law at work.

None of these caveats are born out by empirical evidence; nor for that matter can they be disproven. The New York Sex Crimes Analysis Unit asserted that only 2 percent of the reported cases were false. But when a study was made of those incidents that reached the criminal courts it was discovered that 73 percent of the rapes that dropped into the misdemeanor class were dismissed because the chief witness either wouldn't appear or had withdrawn the charge.

Corroboration rules are one of the more misunderstood elements in criminal law. They do not mean that absolute proof of the complainant's testimony must be submitted. Instead, corroboration requirements call for additional material that *tends* to support the word of the witness.

The judicial attitudes on authentication of testimony in sex cases is clearly articulated in *Coltrane* v. *United States*, a 1969 decision that actually involved conviction of a man for homosexual relations with a

15-year-old boy. "In a long line of decisions we have consistently held that corroboration of the testimony of complainants in so-called sex cases is an indispensable prerequisite to conviction, and for the cogent reason that for these offenses the risk of unjust conviction is high."

The Coltrane opinion continues: "What aspects of the complainant's version must be confirmed? What may serve to adequately corroborate them? In responding to these questions, we try to steer between the Scylla of a corroboration requirement incapable of attainment and the Charybdis of gutting the corroboration safeguard." Appropriately enough, the male justices went to female demon spirits of mythology for the twin dangers.

Steering clear of Scylla—"a corroboration requirement incapable of attainment"—*Kidwell* v. *United States*, in 1912, sanctified convictions where, "the circumstances surrounding the parties at the time were such as to point to the probable guilt of the accused, or, at least corroborated indirectly the testimony of the prosecutrix." Some 30 years after the Kidwell ruling, the defendant in *Ewing* v. *United States* attempted to substitute for the Kidwell yardstick, "direct corroboration of the prosecutrix." It was rejected, explained the Coltrane opinion for it meant testimony of an eyewitness. The Court said, "The result would be in most cases that conviction would not be had except upon the defendant's confession."

The opinion in the Coltrane case summed up as follows: "Corroboration need not be 'direct'—that is, eyewitness—testimony; circumstantial evidence may suffice. Much less need corroboration, as distinguished from the evidence as a whole, connote guilty beyond a reasonable doubt, or even by a preponderance. It suffices that there are 'circumstances' in proof which tend to support the prosecutrix's story and in each case the corroboration 'must be evaluated on its own merits' " [by the jury].

The most obvious form of corroboration would be an eyewitness, a third party's view of the action. A husband forced to watch a man gaining carnal knowledge of his wife while the assailant held a pistol is direct corroboration. That sufficed in the case of the navy watch cap masked burglars. But circumstances— a victim heard to scream for help, torn clothes, disheveled appearance, a ransacked bedroom, bruises and cuts all add up to corroboration.

Still, a woman looking down the barrel of a .32 caliber revolver may very well quietly undress herself, submit without resistance and after the rapist has fled, be unable to demonstrate any corroborative material. The demand for this kind of supportive information, most strongly made in New York until 1974, limits prosecution for rape all along the enforcement process. The cops and the D.A. who first investigate the case may feel that because they cannot develop evidence of force there is no point in pursuing the matter. Even if they make a valiant try and are able to arrest the man the case may be bounced from court by the preliminary hearing judge on the grounds that the law's requirements have not been satisfied. Finally, even if they succeed in bringing the man to trial, the defense may use insufficient corroboration to win a directed verdict of acquittal or build an appeal that brings a reversal of a conviction by a higher court. Judges in some courts must specifically raise the issue of supportive evidence in the charge to the jury.

In jurisdictions such as New York, corroboration on lack of consent or force was structured into the law. Case law in other states serves the same function. When the Nebraska Supreme Court asked that the resistance "must be in good faith, and must persist until the offense is committed," it established a precedent for proof that the offender was threatening enough to cow the woman into submission.

However, evidence of sexual contact or opportunity alone won't convince the law. *State* v. *Dalton* in Missouri accepted that the defendant entered the bed of the complaining witness, "and while there took indecent liberties with her," [but this] is insufficient to justify conviction, since penetration is not shown.

As late as 1927, states such as Ohio clung to a 1781 English Common Law precept that a finding of rape required not only penetration but emission as well. The latter prerequisite may have led to the exclusion of boys under 14 from culpability for rape. While the British retained this feature in their law, American lawmakers came to regard the 14-and-under group as more able. Some courts demanded proof that the youth in question could not demonstrate the powers of the adult male and Louisiana announced full faith in adolescents. Unless otherwise shown, it would not presume incapacity on the part of a young boy. The sternness of Louisiana may have come from the Southern predilection for prosecuting blacks on rape charges.

In New York State, the penetration aspect became easier to prove by revision of the law in 1972. Verification of actual copulation became no longer necessary. A presumption could follow upon the discovery of semen on the underwear of the victim or upon other circumstanial evidence.

People v. *Anthony* in 1944 in New York Supreme Court, Appellate Division, reaffirmed that pregnancy cannot be offered as corroboration of rape. "It is of course highly satisfactory evidence of the guilt of someone," a judicial opinion noted, "but it does not tend to connect a defendant with the commission of the crime." The conviction of Anthony, incidentally, was overturned for the appeal had been based upon the failure of the trial judge to instruct the jury *not* to accept the pregnancy of the victim as supportive.

A third element for which New York insisted upon corroboration was the identity of the accused. To finger the man in a lineup of suspects was not sufficient. A third party had to have seen him enter the apartment or abduct the woman, or, possibly, if a wallet dropped by him could be produced, or some fibers from his jacket found on the scene, that would be regarded as tending to connect him to the crime. It was the most difficult of the corroboration rules to satisfy and it, too, disappeared from the law in 1972. At that, some individuals involved in rape jurisprudence decried its disappearance. "I have a client who has spent eleven months in jail," said Carol Halprin, a Legal Aid Society lawyer. "A sixty-eight-year-old woman accused him of rape; there's no question that she was really raped, it was brutal. But she identified this man as the guy who was a guard in a supermarket. Apparently, the man who raped her wore some kind of a uniform and she remembers a man in uniform at the supermarket who helped her bring her bundles home and then left. She says he returned half an hour later and raped her. It doesn't make any sense that he went with her, came back to the store and then returned to rape her. This is a guy with a family, five children, never been in trouble. If we still had that requirement for corroboration on identification, he would never have been arraigned and sent to jail."

The New York modification on identification extended only to forcible rape. Where force was not the criminal element, as in consensual sodomy or a case in which a child was sexually abused, the old stipulation of corroboration remained.

While the 1967 effort by New York law writers created almost ideal working conditions for rapists—presumably the legislators sincerely thought of themselves as defenders of civil liberties—there was one major change for the worse, so far as the offender was concerned. Until that time the corroborative aspects of a rape case were irrevocably yoked to any felony committed in conjunction with the sexual offense. Rape became not only an escape hatch for compound felonies, but was seemingly encouraged as a way to beat the rap. If, for example, in the course of robbing a house, the bandit paused to rape the householder, it then became necessary for for the cops to have corroborative evidence to cover not only the rape but the robbery as well. In a reverse fashion, the principle surfaced in *People* v. *Florio* (New York Court of Appeals, 1950), an appeal for a conviction on counts of kidnapping as well as rape. The appellants petitioned the higher courts that while they had indeed been guilty of rape as charged, the additional count of kidnapping was unmerited. No corroboration of kidnapping had been introduced, which counsel said was required under the compound felony arrangement. The higher court, while confirming the letter of the law, rejected the Florio petition on the grounds that the circumstances of the rape itself (a girl forced into an automobile and then driven to a desolate place to be violated), fulfilled any need to corroborate kidnapping. Other felons, however, achieved freedom through the compound rule.

The change in 1967, which separated the requirements for proof of one crime from another committed on the same occasion, failed to satisfy growing feminine militancy. A *New York Times* story carried the headline, "*Q:* If a Man Rapes You and Steals Your Television Set, What Can They Get Him For? *A:* Stealing a Television." To have increased the jeopardy for theft of property and not to extend the risk to a form of assault upon an individual seemed almost worse than the previous condition, tantamount to a decision to increase research into the causes of athlete's foot and hold down studies of cancer. Still, under the old law the cops could not have gotten him for either crime.

As with so much of the law, a concise definition by

the *Corpus* of what constitutes corroboration, "some fact or circumstance independent of the witness's testimony" pins the issue down about as well as "Operation Candor" settled all the questions about President Nixon and the Watergaters. Consider the case of the Englishwoman, sitting in the Jamaica, Long Island, railroad station at 3 A.M. after missing the last train to New York City. She was, according to the trial record, a graduate of Oxford University and a student of botany working at a scientific research institute. While at the Jamaica Station she was approached by Peter X, a young man who allegedly invited her to share a cup of coffee with him. When they reached the nearby restaurant, Mr. X informed her that the place "was shutting up." He led her to the back entrance where he grabbed her. She endeavored to pull free, lashing out at X, who bore an injured arm in a sling. He managed to evade her swings, possibly because he was a "professional pugilist," observed the court record.

Four male acquaintances appeared and supposedly helped drag the woman to a nearby car and drove to a shack where all of them had intercourse with her, "some by the back, and some by the mouth." At about 6 A.M. she appeared back in the railroad station looking quite disheveled. She reported her experience to a railroad employee and then, on arriving home, to a married coemployee. A physician tried to examine her, but was thwarted temporarily because she was so nervous he felt obliged to sedate her. "Ensuing medical examination disclosed that force inconsistent with normal intercourse had been exerted."

Peter X and his companions were arrested. Their

92

defense was that she had been a willing participant in sex play. The jury chose not to believe them and brought a guilty verdict. The case was then appealed, on the grounds that the legal requirement of corroboration of force had not been demonstrated. The appeals court justices agreed, with Judge Carswell commenting, "the defendants are of an unworthy type" (Peter X had a record for sodomy and vagrancy and his associates possessed similar police-issued credentials). "But," continued Judge Carswell, "the law is to be applied to the worthy and the unworthy.

"The complainant was of mature age. She was not an inexperienced person. She left a place of safety on the invitation of one of the defendants whose arm was in a sling . . . on her own story her subsequent disclosure [that] she was not unaware of the defendant's purpose and in the successive stages she indicated that she was too cooperative to be the victim of a rape. She apparently acquiesced in or welcomed his conduct. She was more concerned with its effect upon the condition of her apparel than she was for her virtue. . . . The law widely recognizes that some complainants are designing or vicious. If it were not for the rule of corroboration, a defendant would be at the mercy of an untruthful, dishonest vicious complainant."

In his dissent another judge asked, "was complainant's resistance prevented by fear of immediate and great bodily harm; second, did she have reasonable cause to believe that such harm would be inflicted upon her?" He answered himself affirmatively. "She became completely paralyzed, speechless and numb."

This case pinpoints the dilemma of how much resistance or outcry can reasonably be expected in the face of a threat; or how the possibility of a threat may be employed to disguise consensual copulation. The jury that focused on the case believed the botanist; the judges, who wrapped their decision in the niceties of the corroboration requirement, obviously believed Peter X's account (although the dissenters thought they discerned sufficient corroboration). Obviously, supportive evidence, too, becomes relative in its weight, even before magistrates.

New York Court of Appeals in 1959 upheld the conviction in *People* v. *Masse* where corroboration pivoted on equally chancy evidence. Neighbors testified that they had seen Masse in the driveway with the victim shortly before the crime occurred and saw both enter the house. Approximately 30 minutes later the victim fled the house and later Masse was observed picking up a jewel box that had been heaved through a window screen out to the driveway. Three males including Masse had been accused of the rape. Masse, in his appeal, protested lack of corroboration for his identity as well as the element of force or resistance.

The court accepted the proof of Masse's participation in light of the eyewitnesses that placed him at the scene. The victim told the jury that in an attempt to drive off her attackers, she had thrown the jewel box at them and it went through the window screen. That was enough to cover resistance. In the eyes of the appeals court, "the surrounding circumstances of the case have sufficient corroborative value to meet the mandate of the statute."

The corroboration aspect of rape has been one of the most controversial issues in modern times, with feminists, some police and prosecutors urging abandonment, while other cops and naturally all defense attorneys plead that it be retained. "Most of the cases are legitimate," said John Taldone, "but it's difficult to tell a woman she's full of shit. You develop a kind of intuitive sense about it, what's a phoney and what isn't. I'm not in favor of seeing the corroboration thing eased. I don't want to see some guy hung up by his girl-friend because she suddenly got mad at him."

"We had a girl claim she was gang raped by fourteen guys," said Bronx Sex Crimes Squad chief, Lieutenant Joe Bausano. "The lab tests come up inconclusive. There's gotta be some semen with that many guys. They couldn't all pull out, or at least there would have been something on her underwear."

"We are encouraging rape with this type of law," said Lieutenant Julia Tucker, the original head of the Sex Crimes Analysis Unit. "We have fewer rape indictments because of the corroboration problem," said Manhattan Assistant District Attorney Leslie Snyder.

In 1974 the corroboration requirements in New York were dropped altogether as a requirement for arrest and indictment. But U.S. jurisprudence does not necessarily produce different results because of procedural changes. In the courts, and particularly where sex crimes are concerned, the problem quite possibly is not the construction of the law but "we the people" who run the show. Corroboration can be removed from the law, but that does not automatically mean a higher rate of convictions, even though there may be more trials. For one must still face the weight of case law, the precedents that will show in both defense lawyers' summations and in judges' charges. Even more determinate will be the attitude of jurors.

Pennsylvania, a state that does not require corroboration, specified, in 1973: "In any prosecution before a jury for an offense under this chapter [sexual offenses], the jury shall be instructed to evaluate the testimony of a victim or complaining witness with special care in view of the emotional involvment of the witness and the difficulty of determining the truth with respect to alleged sexual activities carried out in private." Less than a year later, the provision, after much criticism, was withdrawn.

More subtle factors than the obligations of the penal code and the instructions of the trial judge enter into the processing of sex offenses. In California, where no pretrial corroboration is required, for example, a Los Angeles prosecutor lost a case in which a 19-year-old secretary was raped in a parking lot. The defendant had been positively identified by a witness to the daylight rape. The D.A. remarked, "all rape cases are hard to prosecute, of course, but this one was so solid." Among the jury that voted to acquit was one who said, "I just couldn't believe that a boy whose girl-friend was as pretty as the one who came into court to testify would have even wanted to rape such a plain-looking girl." What made the reasoning even more looney was that the defendant had been acquitted, nine days before the secretary had been raped, of assault with attempt to rape and had carried a gun to effect his purpose. Such information was, of course, inadmissable at the second trial.

Leslie Snyder spoke of one of her cases, one that ended with a hung jury which voted 10–2 for conviction. The defendant was black, and one of the minority jurors, who was also black, remarked during deliberations that any women who had been raped must have asked for it.

Legal Aid Society lawyers, who defend a majority of those accused of the crime of rape think differently. "Corroboration allows the cops to get rid of the garbage cases, the ones they know are phoney, in a nice way. They can say to a woman, 'Our hands are tied because of the law,' instead of saying you weren't raped. And the same goes for judges who can cite the law and for district attorneys who can look as if they really tried."

Need for corroboration extends into three other kinds of criminal testimony: that for perjury, treason or of being an accessory to a crime. Supportive information is not required for any violent crime, other than rape. In order to understand why there should be any special consideration for the word of the prosecutrix, compare the situation to one in which an accomplice to a crime is put into the witness chair.

A Brooklyn D.A., who strenuously opposes corroboration for rape cases explained: "There are good reasons for requiring validation of the word of an accomplice. He presumably expects to gain some advantage as a result of his testimony. The jury has a right to hear material that supports or destroys his word because he may expect a lesser sentence for his part in the crime. I suppose the reasoning with a woman is that she wants to escape the opprobioum of society by showing that she was forced to engage in a sexual act. On the other hand she doesn't seem to have anything to gain by feigning she is the victim of a robbery or of assault and battery. But I don't believe that women frivolously bring charges of rape, either out of revenge motives or to cover up some indiscretion on their part."

Carol Halprin, of the Legal Aid Society, replied, "You may like to think of this as a rational, logical world but sex just isn't that logical. People do have all sorts of hangups with sex and it is used as a weapon. Our experience is that the charge of rape is a weapon used often by women who have no other means to deal with a guy who is giving them a hard time."

Nobody thinks homicide, atrocious assault and robbery lie beyond the range of human behavior. When the question becomes one of rape, however, the perception of the crime itself seems to be buried under a pile of notions, some of which are facts and some only fables.

V

Fables and Facts

It's Bigger Thomas, Richard Wright's black chauffeur, tempted by the young white woman, rape and murder. It's some monstrous black, bestial wide nostrils, thick lips, lurking in the shadows, ready to drag off the white matron. Or maybe it's Eldridge Cleaver: "I became a rapist. To refine my technique and *modus operandi*, I started out by practicing on black girls in the ghetto —in the black ghetto where deeds appear not as aberrations or deviations from the norm. . . . Rape was an insurrectionary act. It delighted me that I was defying and trampling on the white man's law, on his system of values, and that I was defiling his women—and this point, I believe, was the most satisfying to me because I was very resentful over the historical fact of how the white man has used the black woman. I felt I was getting revenge. From the the site of the act of rape, consternation spreads outwardly in concentric circles.

. . . I came upon a quotation from one of LeRoi Jones's poems. . . .

A cult of death need of the simple striking arm
under the street lamp.
The cutters from under their rented earth. Come
up, black dada nihilismus.
Rape the white girls. Rape their fathers. Cut the
mothers' throats.

". . . many young blacks out there right now are slitting white throats and raping the white girl. They are not doing this because they read LeRoi Jones's poetry as some of his critics seem to believe. Rather LeRoi is expressing the funky facts of life."

Or is it across the tracks where those good ole country boys are just out to have some fun when along comes this nigger gal on the way home from a night-time Bible class, remembrances of times past when *droit du seigneur* of the plantations extended to every white Southerner? Maybe it's a freight car full of young black hoboes, hauled off a train near Scottsboro, Alabama, on the incitement of a pair of white sluts. Can it be good old Charlie, the roomer upstairs who thinks that nubile Alma deserves his special initiation into the rites of womanhood? Is it the street gangs who earn their bones by gang shagging a Hispanic school girl? Is it singles-bar Harold and pickup Molly, one man's seduction, one woman's rape? How about Hitchcock's produce man, garrot first, then thrust home second? Or could it be Ann on the couch, with Byron beside, she whispering "I'll ne'er consent," then consents, but later changes her mind?

At least as basic to the biases about rape is the question of its prevalence. "Whenever we investigate a rape," said one sex crimes cop, "we turn up as many as half a dozen other rapes in the same neighborhood, never been reported." Another sleuth working the same territory says, "I think we hear about every legitimate rape that occurs. Once maybe people were reluctant to come forward, but attitudes have changed. These people want justice and they tell us when a crime has occured."

"Rape is generally conceded to be the most underreported crime," said a police patrol guide.

"The cops treat the woman like she provoked it; the defense attorney makes the woman look like a whore and the courts let the rapists walk out on a technicality. As a result, women are reluctant to come forward," said a feminist.

Who has been doing what unto whom and how often and what has been the result? The statistical cupboard is not quite bare but short rations on substance holds for rape figures. One of the few efforts to seek facts was made by an Israeli sociologist, Menachim Amir who examined 646 incidents determined by the Philadelphia police to be rapes. The two years involved were 1958 and 1960 and 1292 offenders turned up in the police records. The discrepancy between 646 cases and 1292 rapists resulted from the incidence of gang rapes.

"Rape, we found," said Amir, "is an intraracial act, especially between Negro men and women." When the Presidential Commission on Law Enforcement and Administration of Justice looked over Chicago's crime for 1965, it too concluded that rape falls into the category of an intraracial crime. The Presidential Commission on Crime in the District of Columbia reported a consistent pattern of segregation in rape and the figures collected in New York City's Sex Crimes Analysis Unit discerned a similar relationship between violated and violator.

Sociologist M. E. Wolfgang, drawing from a study of victimization for St. Louis, Chicago, Birmingham and North Carolina concluded, "These findings leave no doubt that criminal homicide, like rape and aggravated assault, is overwhelmingly an intraracial phenomonon."

Moreover, the race part of intraracial rape turns out to be basically black. Ceil Jacobs, a graduate student, analyzing the Wolfgang material said, "It is concluded . . . that whites are much less likely than blacks to be victims of rape; black women being the most likely victims of forcible rape. Furthermore, a black or white female has most to fear from a person of her own race in terms of forcible rape." Detective Taldone at the sex crimes squad room, without resorting to a computer printout, said, "It's black on black." The Eldridge Cleavers of the world appear statistically left at the post by those inclined to rapine closer to home.

Crime figures bear some built-in bias, however, and those on rape are no exception. Antisocial behavior victimizes mostly the lower socioeconomic classes (an academic term that disguises the fact that one is talking of the nonwhite ghetto). At the bottom of the pile in Philadelphia, New York, Chicago, Washington, D.C., St. Louis and in fact all points covered by the research squads was the nonwhite underclass of America. Menachem Amir didn't place rape in the genetic tree of the nonwhites but ascribed its prevalence to a subculture of violence among blacks. That's not a very useful interpretation; 18th-Century England teemed with lower-class violence as the *Newgate* and *Tyeburn Calendars* instruct us. At the turn of the 20th Century, when blacks made up a negligible portion of New York's population, large sections of the city never saw a policeman. Some areas, like the notorious Five Points, were considered too dangerous for even armed representatives of the law.

A more serious potential distortion of the racial involvement in rape lies in the dependence upon police data for one's conclusions. A critique of Amir by Betty Mintz in the *Criminal Law Bulletin* insists, "Statistics on rape are clearly affected by the inclusion of unclear or unsolved cases, particularly when it is known that rape is 'one of the most falsely reported crimes.'"

Ms. Mintz remarked, "The high correlation between rape and race of the offender does not, of course, prove that race is the relevant variable. An alternative theory is that it is lower-class members of society in the crowded inner city, regardless of race, who have a high rate of rape arrest." Since so many core cities now house masses of lower-class blacks, it still works out that rape, as a phenomenon of the last 15 years, appears to be largely intraracial, and mostly black on black. Willie Sutton robbed banks because that was where they kept the money. Blacks rape blacks because they are the available females.

The Philadelphia story indicated that 76.9 percent

of the rapes were black on black, 16.3 percent white on white, 3.3 percent black on white and 3.6 percent white on black. A survey of rape in the District of Columbia for an 18-month period in 1969–1970 showed 76 percent black male/black female, 3 percent white male/white female, 21 percent black male/white female and 0.4 percent white male/black female.

The National Commission on the Causes of Prevention of Violence looked over the year 1967 using a random sample of cases from 17 cities. It tabulated: black male/black female, 60 percent; white male/-white female, 30 percent; black male/white female, 10.5 percent; white male/black female, 0.3 percent. The differences may comfortably be ascribed to the composition of the cities. Philadelphia and Washington, D.C. have the largest black populations while some of the cities studied by the NCCPV have more white residents. Philadelphia's Center for Rape Concern, in its 1972 and 1973 experience, found black on white rape up to 20 percent of the incidence. Patterns may be shifting as the population becomes more desegregated and superhighways open up the suburbs to inner-city criminals.

Michael Agopian, a social scientist plumbing the action in Oakland, California, offered an interesting comment about the low number of white on black offenses. "No black woman would report being raped by a white man to the police in Oakland. They might report it to the Panthers but never the police." That phenomenon might hold up in the Panther capital but is hardly likely to be prevalent elsewhere. In a similar sense, Wolfgang discovered, in a study of rape and capital punishment in Arkansas, of a small sample of 55 crimes, not a single white was convicted of raping a black until the 1960s. The chances of white on black rape coming up in police statistics was as likely as Martin Luther King, Jr. being inducted as a Kleagle.

If the preliminary evidence is to be believed, and it too is based largely upon interviews and information requisitioned from the maw of cop research, the rapist comes not as a stranger, or at least not as a total stranger. In nearly 60 percent of Philadelphia's black intraracial rapes, victims and offender knew one another previously. For white on white the figure climbed to 65 percent. In Washington, D.C. almost two-thirds of the total number of victims were attacked by persons with whom they were at least casually acquainted. A Detroit investigation in 1950 came up with better than 50 percent of the participants having a prior relationship. Legal Aid Society lawyers relying on personal experience concur: "In criminal court," said trial lawyer Carol Halprin, "I don't remember a single case where the victims did not know the perpetrator." That may only reflect the major run of cases that get to court; it is easiest to get indictments and to try those cases in which the defilee knows the defiler.

The latest figures gathered by the New York City Sex Crimes Analysis Unit suggest that either patterns are changing, that previous statistics are flawed or New York is unique. The count of connection between the parties to a rape for the first nine months of 1973 showed:

Relatives	37
Girl-friend/Boy-friend	12
Friend, Social Acquaintance	40
Drinking Companion	7
Business Relationship	10
Neighbor	25
Incest	81
Name Known to Victim	622
School Known	2
Seen in Neighborhood	4
No Previous Relationship	98
Other Relationship	53
No Known Relationship	2724

"No known relationship" accounts for better than two-thirds of the cases. Before leaping to any quick conclusion, one must incorporate the frustration quotient for all police figures. The distinction between "no previous relationship, 98" and "no known relationship, 2724" is shaky. The computations depend upon the information fed into the unit. An indifferent investigating officer will fail to pursue the relationship between the parties. Until 1974, New York, in its good-guy rule, usually did not specify race for victims. (The laudable intention of "We don't discriminate," makes for muddled statistics.) As a result, New York cannot offer any data on whether rape is intra- or interracial (offenders' race was reported only because it is an aid in apprehension).

It's not just a matter of quantity; quality enters into the question as well. New York at least broke down the relationship between the concerned pair into shades of acquaintanceship. The reports from Philadelphia are not nearly so subtle. A vaguely recalled face from the street does not compare to the kinship with the neighbor who occupied the apartment across the corridor.

The question of previous relationship becomes an issue because of suspicion of "victim-precipitated rape," provocative acts of the female that either unloosed the irrepressible beast or flashed a misinterpreted signal. Amir described a number of Philadelphia rapes as victim precipitated. He defined these as ones in which the woman inserted herself into a sexually charged situation; the man misunderstood her behavior and responded with a criminal excess of vigor. Women with a reputation for promiscuity or with police records for sexual misconduct (30 percent of the total of Philadelphia rape victims) played the protagonist in these scenes. Misleading semaphores included hanging out in a bar, attendance at a Bacchanalian party, use of "indecent language." Amir theorized that it could be a factor in 40 percent of the cases. The Israeli investigator particularly pinpointed this situation for white on white rape. He noted that, most commonly, the relationship between violator and violated commenced shortly before the offense, like at a saloon or a party.

To the certified male chauvinist sexist pig, the victim-precipitated syndrome proves that a generous number of rapes actually were caused by the victim. A psychiatrist who treated a woman victim said, "She invited rape. She was hitchhiking at four in the morning." A New York criminal courts judge lectured,

"Let's face it, if you're going to wear very short skirts, and sit in a certain way you will invite a kind of reaction."

What about the well-dressed man who carries $200 in cash while walking through a high-crime district? When he is stuck up, does anyone say that it wasn't really robbery, that he provoked the crime by carrying money on his person in a dangerous neighborhood? He may have been ill-advised in behavior but the crime remains robbery, and the thief will be prosecuted. Businessmen can carry traveler's checks or credit cards and leave the valuables in the bank. But what the rapist seeks can't be left at home stored in a vault or secured, without resort to medieval ways of safeguarding virtue. The chief value of "victim-precipitated" findings are cautionaries to women, to be careful what they say to whom and where. The precipitation factors, however, are not licenses for men seeking some quick sexual release.

Forgetting for the moment the excuse of the seduction that *ex post facto* became rape, Philadelphia offers other strange leads about its unbrotherly love. In about 70 percent of the cases, the criminal plotted his act well in advance and another 11 percent were partially planned. That fact alone destroys the concept of invited rape as the basic nature of the crime. A flash of high inside the thighs by female design does not qualify as an invitation for coital attentions two weeks later. The Institute for Sex Research, an organization popularized by the late Dr. Alfred Kinsey, surveyed sex offenders. The studies showed premeditation by

70 percent of the "heterosexual aggressors." The individual victim may be able to reduce her risk by control of her behavior, but obviously the offender already stalks her with overflowingly girded loins.

"An autopsy disclosed that the victim had been strangled and stabbed three times and that she had been sexually assaulted at about the same time that she was killed"—from *The New York Times*. Rape falls into the category of "violent crime." But apart from the element of force that defines the act as sexual intercourse without the consent or against the will, how much actual physical force or violence is employed?

"Most of them don't really beat women up," said John Taldone. "Usually, it is just enough to threaten. We had one rapist who would say, 'If you don't give me what I want, I'll hurt your children.' You have to remember, the person is taken unaware, she's too stunned to react, and if he's got a knife or gun—."

The staff report of the National Commission on the Causes and Prevention of Violence stated that only 21 percent of the rape victims were hurt in ways beyond the act itself. And a study at the Philadelphia General Hospital found that 18 of 50 victims were assaulted as well as raped. New York's most recent findings show about 50 percent of the women on the receiving end of brute force.

Amir, however, sketched a fairly bloody and bruised anatomy of Philadelphia victims. About 30 percent received either brutal beatings or choking. An additional 50 percent he called "beaten, not brutally." The fine distinction between rough handling and brutality depended upon whether the injuries required medical treatment.

The most phantasmic bogey man is the sadorapist, the psychotic who gets his jollies out of carving up the victims, putting lighted cigarettes to their breasts, throttling them before or after he consummates the act. The Kinsey research team went through a sample of 18,000 people without finding a single reported experience with a sexual sadist. The prevailing view of the cops is that the amount of physical violence employed by the rapist is directly proportionate to the resistance of the victim. It is still a no-win game for the recipient. Resistance means lumps on the head, a bloody nose, a broken tooth, a split lip or assorted fractures. Passive compliance engenders suspicion in law-enforcement officials that the visitation was not unwelcome, or else makes the case a difficult one to prosecute. Determined resistance can cause what the CIA labels "termination with extreme prejudice." Death and rape generally coincide if the woman puts up too much of a fight or if the offender panics and wishes to make identification and capture more difficult.

As Taldone observed, many women appear either so stunned or frightened that they lose the ability to react. The verbal threat was enough. With a minimum of 40 million handguns in the hands of Americans, knives no further away than the kitchen if the intruder carelessly forgot his own, the obligation of resistance takes on the absurdity of a strict code for prisoners of war when the brainwash factories have achieved such a sophisticated level. Blackstone's advice that the justice system be wary if the victim fail to cry out becomes as obsolete as trial by ordeal. Bullets travel quicker than a yell for help, which in today's urban climate goes unheard or unheeded anyway. Blackstone erected his pyramid of precedents long before the designers of modern ordnance and the geniuses of manufacture combined to make portable guns cheaply and keep them freely circulating. Conceivably, even a Blackstone might offer some out for a woman faced with a pistol-toting man of unrestrained lust.

The time and the place for rape appear fairly commonplace. The National Commission's survey of forcible rape in Chicago discovered that half the women were raped within a home, not necessarily their own. Figures ran slightly higher for whites compared to blacks. The second choice for rape in Chicago was the street. In Philadelphia, the residential setting was the basic site of black operations; whites performed more often in automobiles. Amir interpreted this as a sign of white affluence but it may have been a natural locale because of the frequency with which white on white rape occured after a meeting at a bar or a party.

In Philadelphia, said Amir, "forcible rape is predominantly a nocturnal crime; it tends to be a weekend, midnight and summer occurrence." Several other cities pinpointed a peak summer rape incidence. However, New York experienced rape as a crime for all seasons; rapists were not busier in summer months than colder ones. For that matter, the New Yorkers worked at their criminal avocation without favoring any day of the week. Your average Brooklyn offender liked Sundays best. In Manhattan, the Sabbath rapes were the second lowest. (No one suggests an invidious comparison between the devotions of Manhattan rapists to the Lord's day and Brooklyn's less observant felons.) In the Bronx, Tuesday found rapists more industrious than on Saturday.

Rough consistency marked the hours of New York rapists. While the four other sections of the city peaked between 1 and 2 A.M., Manhattanites, perhaps because of livelier and later nighttime recreations, did more of their raping between 3 and 4 A.M. Between 6 A.M. and noon, the majority of sex offenders either lay abed, breakfasted, worked or else found themselves hard put to find opportunities. In Manhattan and the Bronx, the pace of sexual offenses quickened by two in the afternoon, while Brooklyn languished until toward 8 P.M. when action again became brisk.

The most difficult fact to ascertain is the volume of forcible rape in America. On the crime charts, forcible rape usually crops up right behind homicide in the listings, which is an indication of how seriously rape is regarded by those who make up the reports.

But departments seeking added men and appropriations have been known to overreport in an effort to create a crisis atmosphere of crime in the streets. On the other hand policemen may undervalue larcenies into lesser crimes, or ignore some assaults if that will lessen the pressure from city hall, or the local press. Then there are those cities in which it is felt that crime statistics somehow aid the criminals. For example, when the Legal Aid Society wrote to the city of Dallas and asked for its figures on rape, Assistant Chief of

Police T. A. Hutson politely replied, "The Dallas Police Department's procedures prohibit the releasing of this information."

Homicide figures come close to a true picture of the actual incidence of murder. There is a body; even a hack medical examiner rarely gets fooled into certification of accidental death. The only leakage occurs in cases of individuals listed as missing, but who have been surreptitiously buried or consigned to the water along with weighty matters. Another accurate crime statistic is auto theft since everyone insures his car and, in order to collect, must report the missing vehicle to the cops. After that it's all quicksand. Burglary, robbery, simple assault, especially in the low-income or nonwhite cores of cities are vastly underreported. Finding a sewing machine or a color TV lifted from Hough in Cleveland, Chicago's South Side or New York's Bedford Stuyvesant would be harder than tracing the movement of a ten-dollar bill dropped off at the Committee to Reelect the President in the days before the federal law demanded accurate record keeping. Cops don't try hard in these cases and the people know that it's hopeless even to make the complaint. In the affluent suburbs, the stolen TV won't be found either, but it's reported to the cops because there's either theft insurance to cover it or a deduction from income tax. Both require police notification of the robbery. The pattern repeats for simple assault and robbery; the violence of the sociologist's "disadvantaged people" draws less than a modicum of concern from the local cops. There's so much of it that they have become inured to anything less than murder and the citizens know it. In the high-rent districts it's different. He who steals by political or business corruption, white-collar polite crime, is properly appalled at anyone who stoops to violence. He calls the cops.

Sex crimes carry their own distorting mirrors. Victims conceal the offense for fear it stains them or exposes them to further ordeals. Some police departments do not list accusations of rape if, in their judgment, the case will not be strong enough to prosecute. Until 1971, Washington, D.C. chose to tabulate rape is this way. Nevertheless a crime had occurred, and it was one that never got into the FBI computer.

According to the Uniform Crime Reports of the United States, compiled by the FBI, reported rapes increased at the same rate as other crimes from 1960–1969. After that year, the rape rate leaped forward ahead of other crimes against the person. Some might construe that the crime itself wasn't actually increasing, only that more women were coming forward. However, some students of the problem, such as Camille E. LeGrande, think differently. In the *California Law Review*, she argued that in view of the increasingly widespread discussion of the futility of rape charges and the humiliations to be suffered by the women who do go to the cops, the reverse ought to have been the case. Ms. LeGrande reports that investigators for California estimate that only 20 percent of all rapes reach the police blotter. Minnesota cops say that perhaps one-quarter of all rapes come to their attention. The President's Commission of Law Enforcement in a Free Society arrived at 27 percent reported of the actual rapes. Other guesses go from one to three to as much as one to ten. Militant feminists like the higher multiple, and so do headline writers. *Philadelphia* magazine took the three rapes reported daily to the cops and titled the article on the subject "30 Rapes A Day."

Although the national figures are up, local statistics offer only spotty confirmation. Los Angeles went from 1988 in 1970, to 2062 in 1971 and 2205 for 1972. During those years homicides in Los Angeles went from 394 to 427 to 501, increasing about twice as fast as forcible rape. Aggravated assault—"attack with an intent to kill or to inflict severe bodily damage by shooting, cutting, stabbing, maiming, scalding, etc., but does not include simple assault and battery or street fighting"—climbed over the period, but not in any steady pattern. Robbery and auto theft both declined from 1971 to 1972 after moving up from 1970.

Jacksonville, Florida reported 349 rape offenses in 1970, 303 in 1971 and 354 in 1972. Pittsburgh listed 246 rapes for 1970, 279 for 1971 and 298 for 1972. Rape incidents on campuses reached such a volume in 1973 that colleges recruited large numbers of guards. Students still said the rapists continue to prey.

Those who believe that society has failed to protect women from rapists concern themselves not only with the offense rates but with the dispostion of cases. "Although rapes tend to be both violent and planned," said Camille LeGrande, "very few apprehended rapists are ever charged with and convicted of rape. . . ." Unfortunately, she depends upon 1967 figures that include statutory rape, sexual offenses with the consent of an underage female. It is, however, true that for the nation as a whole, convictions for accusations of rape fell below the average for convictions on all other felonies brought to trial. Where the penal code has made for sticky going, as in New York, D.A.s are happier to plea bargain, drop the sex-crime charge, if the man will accept a burglary rap. Feminists picketed after a D.A. accepted a guilty plea on another felony (with a stiff jail term) and dismissed the rape charges.

The city of Detroit arrested 388 individuals for rape in 1972. The number actually to go on trial amounted to only 142, and of these 53 were convicted, 35 acquitted and 55 were held over. It works out to a conviction rate of better than 35 percent for those tried, but based on arrests the number found guilty amounts to about 14 percent. Columbus, Ohio, arrested 109 men for rape in 1972 and convicted nine on that charge and 12 on lesser offenses, while 41 were acquitted or dismissed. The rest went to juvenile courts or were still pending. However one totes it up, the number of people incarcerated for rape figures out to be minute. Nationwide, the FBI shows a disposition of rape prosecutions for 1972 as 49 percent dismissed, 32 percent found guilty and 19 convicted of lesser offenses.

No clear relationship between the effect of corroboration upon the rate of convictions appears. Two states that have the corroboration restriction, Georgia and Iowa, averaged well over the national figure while New York, with similar regulations, fell far below. Worth noting, for New York, was that after 1972 the lessening of the demands for additional evidence resulted in a drop from dismissals for rape from 60 to

40 percent. That still, however, put the sex-crime dismissal level way over the rate for all felonies, which was only 10 percent of the cases brought into court.

For the victim who decides to brave the slings and arrows of all those people who will look at her suspiciously when she confesses to having been raped, the prospect of judicial satisfaction seems somewhat dim. And for the rapist, who like the Chicago killer perhaps pleads, "stop me before I do it again," the expectation of apprehension, punishment and treatment, seem equally poor. But then, does he really want to be reprogrammed into sexually acceptable behavior? Is he abnormal and for that matter will the woman truly suffer calumny because she dares admit that she was a victim?

"You know I'm not sure I understand rape at all," said a defense lawyer. "I don't know why a man would want to rape a woman who doesn't want it and I don't see how a woman can be penetrated if she doesn't cooperate. You just can't thread a moving needle."

During the trial of a man who was accused of raping two women in hallways, the defense attorney questioned the possibility of rape on physiological grounds, whether intercourse can be accomplished without cooperation from the woman. "A woman has to at least be willing to raise her leg and wrap it around the man."

Behind the doubts of these counselors is the problem of how many false rape charges are filed. The Sex Crimes Analysis Unit in New York puts the unfounded at only 2 percent. That figure, however, does not include those instances where the original investigating officer refused to accept the claim of a rape and filed the case as unfounded. Defense lawyers, and some male cops, claim that phoney rapes, charges made out of revenge, anger and sheer perversity add up to more than 2 percent. "Among the poor," said Carol Halprin, "calling the cops on a guy is one of the few ways if not the only way to punish him."

Even if the rape claim gets beyond the initial jaundiced eye of detectives it may turn out subsequently to have been something other than what was asserted. "At the preliminary hearing," said Carol Halprin, "I always ask the question, 'After the rape was completed, how long before he left?' In one case, she answered, 'About forty-five minutes.' I asked what happened during this time. She said, 'We played some records, drank a beer.' The judge at the preliminary hearing threw the case out of court." A spurious charge dismissed by a magistrate does not count in the 2 percent of unfoundeds listed officially by the cops.

Even granting the low figure of 2 percent there remains the dilemma of whether it is better to conduct the judicial process in a manner which makes it easier to prosecute the real offenders and simultaneously puts away a handful of innocent men, or, is it better if 100 guilty go free as long as one innocent is not imprisoned? A woman active in New York Women Against Rape growled, "To hell with the 2 percent, I think it's time to worry about the 100 women." It's not your civil libertarian viewpoint, but then it is the women who have had to pay the price to the rapist.

VI

Tales of the Victims

Martha Eames was awakened by a noise at about 4:30 in the morning. At the large French-style window of the ground floor apartment she saw a figure. It hesitated for perhaps 30 seconds. In that interval, Martha Eames loosed a single darkness piercing scream. "He came quickly to the bed then," remembered Martha Eames. "He looked like he was enormous in size; maybe it was just the light that made him appear so massive but I felt such primal terror that I was unable to yell again or to resist. You just cannot imagine how terrifying it was, how overwhelming. I think it must be something like the sensation of an infant shortly after birth when it becomes hungry and it does not know that it will be fed. Until it receives a bottle or the breast it must be panicked with a primal fear. It's not just the rape or the intercourse itself. I could accept that. There's the dread of being hurt, of being killed."

Did he have a weapon? "His penis was his weapon. Oh, he also had a stainless steel Afro pick [a comb with a pointed end]. He wasn't physically brutal, but never the less I was just so stunned with terror. Resist? What was the point? Face it. A man like that was so much stronger than I, I'm only a hundred and five pounds, he must have been close to two hundred.

"When he finished, the first time, he just lay there beside me in the bed, stroking my body. He came on very easy with a soft-spoken voice. He asked me if this was the first time that this had ever happened to me. He asked me how I felt. I kept giving brief answers.

"He asked me if I was married and I said yes. I had been, but I was divorced. The man I had been living with had recently moved out. He immediately jumped up to check the closet and he found only my clothes. He said, 'you're lying.' I said, 'Look in the closet in the bathroom.' There were still a few things left from the guy who had been living with me. He said, 'There's not much here.' I said, 'My husband's been on a trip for a while.'

"He sat down and started to talk some more. Much of my training has been in psychology and I have worked for psychiatrists and with people with emotional problems. I felt I was dealing with a man who had performed a most irrational act. I said, 'You don't have to do this sort of thing.' I said, 'What would you have done if there had been someone here, a man, a man with maybe a gun?' He told me that was why he waited at the window until I awakened. If he saw two heads pop up he would have left.

"I said it wasn't worth going to jail to do this. That

got me into a sort of trap. He immediately asked if I had any money. He said he really didn't want to rob me, that he'd pay me back because robbery wasn't really his thing.

"I got my wallet which had only a few dollars in it. He asked, 'Is that all you've got?' My terror increased; he'd already checked me out on whether I had a husband by looking through the closet and if he found out I held out on money I might be in worse trouble. I went back and got the fifty dollars I'd just drawn from the bank and hidden in a drawer.

"I was still dazed and naked. He looked around and saw some bottles on a shelf. He said, 'Is that real liquor? Can I have a drink?' There was no way for me to say no, but again he was very careful about touching things. He didn't want to handle the bottle. He ordered, 'you pour it for me.'

"I was still shaking and he continued to ask questions like whether this had ever happened to me. He said we now had a special kind of relationship. He also told me that he had to be careful because he had done time. I asked him if it was for rape and he said no, but I found out it was for attempted rape. He was standing by the sideboard with the liquor and I could see that he was also standing where all of my kitchen knives were hanging.

"While he was standing there he went into a long speech about his trial. Then he told me that he had a problem, he liked to drink. But outside of smoking pot or maybe sniffing coke, he would have nothing to do with drugs. He said the idea of injecting something into his body was something he disliked; it was an invasion of the body. Which was weird considering what he had done to me.

"He told me he had a thing for white women when he got high. I said that an analyst whom I worked for had handled this type of problem. Maybe he could help him. But he answered, 'he's not you.' He said he'd been married and separated, had lived with a white woman who 'tried to raise me up,' but he preferred to be himself, he claimed.

"About this time, I said I wanted to go to the bathroom. He let me, and in there I put on a robe. He talked some more about prison, saying that the people there put down the muggers and junkies. He didn't say anything about how they regarded sex offenders.

"I sat down on the bed and he held my feet gently, on a hassock. He said, could he maybe call me after this was over, but he'd have to be careful because he didn't want anything to do with 'New York's finest.' I told him the number and he got up and checked it out against the phone. He asked if I had any credit cards. I told him that would be just a real pain in the ass. Because, I would just call up and say they had all been stolen and he might get picked up because he had my cards. He still wanted to see a credit card. I took my Master Charge from my wallet and gave it to him. He really wanted it only for my name, I guess, because he read it aloud, then gave the card back, after carefully wiping off his fingerprints.

"He held my feet again and he noticed a blister on a toe. He touched it gently, and asked how it happened and I told him it was from a shoe. He kissed the blister and then put his hand up my robe. Oh, Christ, I thought, again.

"I tried to give excuses. I said it's getting light out, the super will come around to take out the garbage. He said it's still too early. I tried firmness. I said I didn't want to. He just pulled me back into the bedroom.

"When he took his clothes off, it was like a performance, everything done in almost slow motion. He said, 'This time it's for you.'

"I closed my eyes at first, tried to blot everything out. Then I forced myself to look. I said to myself I should remember, remember everything about his face. I had blacked out his face until now. As a matter of fact, he had raped a girl in the same building a few days before and she had blacked out his face so well that she could not identify him.

"I told myself I was not consenting. He may have been gentle, he may have considered that he was making love to me, but I had not consented.

"When he finished, I said, 'Now will you please go?'

"Instead, he said, 'Could I take a shower?'

"I was so exhausted, I said 'Yeah, why not.' He was very brief in the shower, and he left the bathroom door open, did not pull the shower curtain. I just didn't think I could risk making a phone call, and I figured he'd leave soon, which was what I desperately wanted.

"I was supercalm when he finally went. I immediately dialed 911 [the emergency number for police in New York]. The cops came right away and took me to

Roosevelt Hospital. A doctor did the vaginal examination, gave me penicillin in case he had V.D. I had a bad reaction to it, but it turned out he did have V.D. and I was glad I had [been given] the penicillin. They also gave me an injection of DES [a synthetic estrogen that prevents conception]. It gave me nausea for several days.

"When I met with the detectives on the case I was still supercool. I had made a list of things that he touched. I described the guy right down to the dirt under his fingernails, everything that he said to me. I remembered that on the middle finger of his left hand he wore a bandage, a professionally applied bandage.

"I spent two-and-a-half hours with a police department artist and he worked up a sketch on the guy. I kept bugging the police to go after the man. A couple of days later, some cops on the anticrime patrol saw a man lurking in the rain, right near the building where I was raped. They thought he might be figuring out how to get into this place. In my case, he had stood on a garbage can to reach up to the window.

"They took him down to the precinct and I sat in that little room with the one-way looking glass. I picked him out immediately. Several other women whom he had attacked also identified him. The corroboration law was still in effect and I couldn't have shown much evidence, except that for all his carefulness he had left fingerprints around my apartment which the police found. In addition, when I screamed while he was at the window, a neighbor [had] heard me, looked out and saw a figure at the window. When the police came, however, they went to the apartment below me and it would have gone as 'unfounded' if I hadn't called.

"I am not conscious that he had followed me. I had never seen him before but he might have seen me since I occasionally would sunbathe by that French window. He had raped the girl next door and maybe he felt that it was an easy building to get into.

"I moved out of the apartment immediately and stayed with some friends. Although I had been super-calm with the police I found myself waking up at four-thirty in the morning, thinking there was a man at the window, even though I was now twenty-five stories off the ground. Even with valium and nembutal, I'd still wake up at four-thirty and suffer that terror. Depression would hit me, like after I spent a long time with the detectives in the apartment, made coffee for all the boys, I suddenly felt very down.

"There were other things that bothered me. I felt that all of the cops I dealt with, however professional they claimed to be in their work, were coming on to me. I sort of felt that they were licking their chops, while they were looking at me. Somebody might say that I was just oversensitive but the cops who deal with a rape victim ought to be supersensitive to the problem, they should have some sensitivity training. Some have, but I think women detectives would already be supersensitive. There's a whole question in my mind of what kind of a man goes on a sex crimes squad; some guys like to chase ass, and do the people in charge make sure this type isn't in such a sensitive job?

"The problems began to hit me harder and harder. I suddenly realized that DES had been linked with cancer. Nobody at the hospital even asked if there was cancer in my family. I thought, my God, if I have a daughter, she might someday come down with vaginal cancer as a result. I was on a subway at the time and I just broke down and bawled at the thought. I went home and called Jeffrey Rovins, [an] assistant D.A. who was handling the case, and yelled at him for not having pushed the case along.

"My friends were very supportive and loving. I would start crying and say 'What's the big deal?' They would say it really is a big deal, and there's nothing wrong in crying about it. At one stage I cried for three straight days. I was becoming confused and I called my former analyst. I didn't have enough money to go into treatment. If I just saw him once I'd probably spend all the time crying. It wouldn't be any good. He suggested that I just try writing down what happened, that basically what I needed was to let all my anger out.

"When I saw him [the rapist] at the arraignment, I thought of what must be going through his mind, prison, maybe the same kind of terror I felt. I guess that's because of my background in psychology. He has this affable manner, it's not an affectation. The cops weren't impressed, they referred to him as that 'son of a bitch.' He had a pocketful of telephone numbers like mine, there must have been many more than the four rapes that the police tied him too.

"That appearance before the grand jury was postponed three times and that took its toll. The detective who was supposed to bring the medical report suddenly realized he'd forgotten to get one. We had to go to the hospital. The doctor was really great, however, he insisted on appearing before the grand jury. Before I went on the stand I felt a little nervous but I had gone over my experience, and I knew what I would have to tell the grand jury.

"When my turn came, I looked out at all those people [23 for a grand jury, plus assorted lawyers, court attendants and a judge]. I opened my mouth to speak. Nothing came out, I just broke down crying and couldn't respond. I was asked if I wanted to take a break, but I said no and finally I became able to answer the questions. He was indicted for both burglary and rape.

"There was no trial, however. He plea bargained and although he resisted it at first, he finally took one count of burglary and one of rape. The judge gave him ten years. But he's eligible for parole after one year, unless that new state law that demands a convicted person serve a minimum of half the sentence holds for him.

"I was very angry at first and went into another depression. But Jeffrey Rovins reminded me that we did get a conviction, and I did not have to go into court. When it was time for him to be sentenced I thought about going to see the judge, to make a statement about what rape meant to a woman, but in the end I decided not to get any further involved. I suppose, like every person who has been wronged I had looked forward to my day in court.

"I don't live in the same place anymore. I never told my father what happened to me and it took maybe six months for me to recover my emotional equilibrium. I kept having fantasies of being killed by men; I went back into analysis, although only partly because of the rape problem. As far as he is concerned, I don't know what to think. I certainly don't want him out on the streets again because he will commit rape again. But I know what prisons are like and he won't get what he needs there either."

Helen Anne, blonde, slim, attractive, stands before a community meeting in the basement of a Brooklyn church and relates her story. To be able to go to the police, to endure their questioning and that of the district attorney, to accept the fact that one becomes a neighborhood curiosity, even perhaps a target for men who see a new sensuality in you because you've been a rape victim, are all painful and difficult, but to get up in front of rooms full of strangers and talk about the crime—that is a sign of new times.

"It was a Friday afternoon. I was living on the West Side of Manhattan near Central Park. I walked into the building vestibule and there he was, a middle-aged white man with a knife. He proceeded to deal with me for fifteen minutes right there. I didn't scream; he had a knife and he didn't cut me. In the midst of the act, a woman entered the vestibule. She disrupted him with her appearance and he took off. I went upstairs, called the police who came quickly. They were patient, kind, maybe I was just lucky in the cops who came to see me.

"After I went to the hospital for an examination, I was taken to the local precinct station. There, the detectives were a little jovial but they didn't seem to be unsympathetic. They asked me what the man looked like. You're so scared when it happens that you don't remember things. Maybe it's a way of tuning out the experience. They asked me if he had a moustache and it was hard for me to recall that he did have one. They showed me some mug shots and there were several men in there who looked something like him. The woman who had frightened him away was at the precinct house. She was no help at all. She was positive he was black. I knew he was white.

"That was all there was to the attempt to find him. I never saw the police again. Maybe that was my fault, partly. I never returned to the apartment. They may have called and been unable to reach me. I moved in with a friend immediately and went looking for another place to live.

"For a while after I was raped, I went through a positively paranoid period. When I walked on the street, I wanted to know who was behind me or on the subway with me. I crossed the street when I saw men whom I thought looked suspicious. I'm better now but there's been a permanent change in the way I live. I try to know the community in which I live and think about where my apartment is. I don't take the area for granted. I know where the stores I use are and I plan my trip to, say the grocery store to make sure that I take a route that is well-lighted or has a lot of traffic, people on it.

"I'm pleased I went to the police, even though nothing happened. I went because I was mad that someone did that to me. I don't have any feeling of shame and I don't think any woman should have one."

Kitty Allen stood up at the same meeting to tell of her terror. "I was asleep in my apartment when I heard a noise. There was a man there. I cannot explain how I felt. The thing was he seemed to want to talk. He even said that he would like to create some sort of a relationship with me.

"If he had had a gun or some weapon, I don't believe I would have been able to think clearly at all. But I had an idea, maybe based on something I had once heard. I told him that because I was so afraid, he couldn't physically enter me. If he really wanted me, maybe we should go out to dinner. We kept talking, for an hour at least. He even smoked. Finally I convinced him that if he would call me, we would make a date and go out. He left, taking with him my telephone number.

"I was hesitant about calling the police. But then I had read an article in *MS.* magazine and so I did. Two nice cops came and interviewed me. Then four of them took to staying in my apartment waiting for him either to show up or call. On the second night he did telephone me. We made a date for him to meet me. And the cops seized him when he appeared.

"I have heard stories where people did not find themselves that lucky in their experience with the police but I certainly can't complain about their behavior.

"I no longer feel that I'm a victim. Now I'm a complainant and I'm pressing the charges. He can't be held for rape but he did fondle me, touch my breasts and that sort of thing. That makes him guilty of sexual abuse. It's a much better feeling than to sit back and try to forget about the thing. Otherwise, there's always some who will say you got what you wanted.

"When I woke and saw him there I felt supreme terror. If you have time, and maybe because he didn't show any weapon, your survival instinct comes on. You think of ways to get out of the situation, I actually had heard of someone who, after she was raped, said, 'Gee, it was great. Why don't you come back again tomorrow night.' When he did, she had policemen there and they grabbed him. That gave me my idea of telling him it would be much more enjoyable under different circumstances.

"Even though I no longer think of myself a victim, in the immediate period after the incident, I did feel different. I felt a lack of sexuality in myself for a month. I suppressed awareness of my body and its desires. At the same time, whenever I was in my apartment, I kept myself covered. I suppose I was trying to avoid any sense of having provoked the man.

"The experience makes you feel you are being punished for being a female. You can't disguise that sensation. You do have a fear of men, a fear of anyone who looks at all like the criminal.

"I actually thought about moving to a new address, getting a male roommate or a big dog. But I liked my place, I liked living by myself. I liked the neighborhood. So I got gates and locks for my shutters.

"For one month I had stayed away, living in the apartments of friends. I don't think there's anyone on my block who didn't know what happened to me. But I did not run across any prejudice, the people around were all outraged and as helpful to me as possible.

"My intellect tells me that this person is sick, the response he wants from me is not normal. He's a mental case and I'd be for that sort of treatment, if I was sure that he'd get competent psychiatric care. But I don't think he should be allowed to spend a few days in jail and then walk the streets again. Unfortunately, in our society, there doesn't seem to be any good alternative. There has to be protection for the individual and society from this criminal.

"One other thought I had after it was over, was getting a gun, legally, to protect me in case he ever came back. But I decided against that. Instead, there's been a development of a sort of community self-protection. It's a high-crime neighborhood. We are arranging a system where after you leave someone's place, you call them upon arriving home safely. I don't know how much good it actually does, but one loses that sense of insecurity."

Several women listening to Kitty Allen volunteered their own urban strategy. "I took a judo course for one year. With what I've learned; my panic reaction has been reversed. Most of us freeze when confronted by an attacker. At the end of my year of training I felt that I would not be afraid. I know I don't have the power of the men on my block but I no longer have to feel myself shrinking in myself when I go out to catch a bus. If someone made a suspicious move, my body moved in my defense. You start to think how much force will I have to use on him rather than how much will I have to accept. You get confidence."

These three managed to keep their heads together. Others simply fall apart.

"It leaves some of them scared shitless," said John Taldone. "They don't want to leave the house even with a police officer. I've had a witness go into convulsions before the grand jury. One thing is that they all want to move."

The trauma becomes particularly devastating to anyone who has had previous emotional problems. A college instructor, the wife of an investment banker, was among the victims of the 315-pound pharmacist and his "nail-hardener" pills. Prior to the assault she had shown signs of instability. She required intensive psychiatric care to get her through the accused's first trial, and when it became obvious that she would have to go through another trial, she fell apart. According to her husband, whenever the subject of the second trial would come up, "She's just a totally different person. She becomes emotionally destroyed . . . she loses all judgment, she becomes totally irrational. She's had rashes, she's become physically violent toward people around her. . . . I still have bruises." When the D.A. confirmed that the victim would have to take another turn on the witness stand, she became so distraught that she nearly burned down the apartment by leaving the gas on, unattended. On the basis of this information, the judge at the second trial excused her from testimony. The pharmacist, a former Notre Dame football player, failed to overturn his original conviction and his two-to-five year term.

Pathetically little research on the effects of rape

upon women has been done. *Victimology*, a new discipline now being fought over by sociologists, psychologists and criminologists, is, as yet, a newborn. The first international conference on the subject was only held in 1973, appropriately enough in Israel. One long-term program of study, begun in 1970, is underway at the Philadelphia General Hospital. It grew out of a project for treatment of probationed sex offenders initiated in 1955.

The protocol in Philadelphia calls for a female social worker to contact the victim within 48 hours after she has been treated in emergency service at the hospital. Arrangements are made for a complete psychiatric workup of the victim. For the next full year the woman is seen regularly by the social worker. The victim is offered psychiatric help if it is judged as being warranted. At the end of the year, in any event, another psychiatric examination helps determine how well the victim has adjusted.

Dr. Joseph Peters, a psychiatrist who started the original program and directs the Philadelphia General Hospital Center for Rape Concern, said, "Although the initial shock of the rape experience is usually coupled with intense concern for the victim, a period of denial of emotional response by both victim and those close to her often follows" (although there may be a period of hysterical reaction immediately after the rape). The victim, apparently, initially musters enough psychological reinforcement to stave off what Dr. Peters describes as an acute situational reaction. But, perhaps a month or so after the incident, the victim collapses into a depression. There's an inability to sleep, changes in appetite. In standard psychological jargon it would be called traumatic neurosis; the problem with this term is that it places a certain amount of the onus upon the victim, just as the term "combat neurosis" (breakdown under wartime stress) places a similar burden upon its sufferer. The phenomenon is consistent with a small study of 13 Vista workers in Boston who were raped. They too reported an initial period of denial and "pseudoadjustment" which was eventually followed by a deep moody blues. Martha Eames, Helen Anne and Kitty Allen all suffered the same pangs.

Just why the reaction appears some weeks later can only be speculated upon by psychiatrists, sociologists and social workers dealing with victims. "Most victims who have had the experience," said a caseworker, "who have been threatened with a gun, knife, pipe or even fists, afterward are glad to have gotten away relatively unharmed. They feel lucky to be alive. The experience of the rape itself only begins to build up after time, the initial fear would seem to be physical pain or death."

Because of the time lag between the crime and the onset of the depression—or "acute situational reaction"—Dr. Peters believes the cause and effect are often not connected. Less well-educated women, or those who do not tend to see events from a psychological perspective, would be particularly unlikely to realize the true source of their distress. In Dr. Peters's view, "Soon after the initial trauma a massive denial involving all parties usually develops. The victim appears emotionally settled. The family is relieved to drop charges. The police and courts, already overburdened and biased with a male viewpoint, are somewhat skeptical about the reliability of the victim's complaints and seem anxious to drop the matter." It would not be surprising, in view of this widespread self-imposed censorship, that the victim does not perceive that the personality change stems from the rape.

"I was fine for a couple of months and then it hit me," said a New York editor who was hustled off the street at gunpoint and raped in the bushes of a nearby park. "Then I felt guilty, became quite depressed, unhappy with everything." Whether the defiled always feel themselves at fault is something that has yet to be sorted out fully by the Philadelphia unit. "I actually don't see a lot of guilt on the conscious level," said one of the psychiatrists in the program. "You do hear comments like, 'I feel dirty,' and 'I'm not the same' or 'Nobody will ever have me.' This last is particularly true for a white girl who has been attacked by a black man."

Reporter Roberta Brandes Gratz of the *New York Post*, wrote a story detailing one of the knottier turns of guilt. Yvette, the victim, living in New York's East Village, was stopped by a young man who said he had just arrived from California. He told Yvette he had been robbed, that his clothes had been stolen and that he needed a crash pad. He solicited her help to vouch for him at a place he had located. The place was down an alley where instead of a pad, it turned out he sought something else. He choked Yvette, banged her head against the cement, raped her, ripped off her watch and ran. What did she do then? "I ran home and washed. I was so ashamed. I just wanted to go home, take a shower and wash away the incident. I blamed myself because I had listened to his rap. My face was all swollen and my body all black and blue and when I walked in my roommates were really horrified. They tried to get me to go to the police or a hospital but I couldn't bring myself to do it. I had heard about the hassles, how police and hospital people never believe you and ask all sorts of incredible questions." Indeed all of these may have helped deter her from seeing the authorities. But what seems paramount is her guilt for having swallowed such a sucker story.

Guilt of another kind nearly drowns the victim in court. Gratz cited another victim's reaction. "At one of the pretrial hearings, the defendant looked so confused and scared. He stood with such a hurt look, like he was the one being victimized. George Whitmore [a celebrated case of a wrong man prosecuted for rape and several spectacular murders] was in the back of my mind. And the courtroom spectators were all glaring at me. I felt so self-conscious and defensive.

"That's why a lot of women like me don't even report a rape. Even my friends were reluctant to see me press charges. I knew if you get a liberal judge, he can go easy on the kid 'cause he's black. I found myself wanting the kind of judge I loathe.

"I just can't throw off the history. I felt like I'm being used to pay off the old debt of black men being falsely accused in the South of raping white women."

It has been suggested that the entire route along which criminal justice crawls inevitably makes a woman feel guilty. The cops who interrogate the chief

witness ask punishing questions. "What were you doing in that neighborhood?" "Is that your normal way
home?" "Did you try to lock all the windows?" "Did
you know him or had you ever seen him before?"
"How much did you resist?" "Did you scream?" "Did
you assist him during intercourse?" The interrogation
becomes accusatory, even inquisitorial.

An angry feminist, advised of this kind of questioning, demanded, "What right have they got to ask why
you were in an area, or whether you always went out
at night alone?" But these and other questions of a
similar nature are necessary for building a case and
not only will they arise in court, but when the defense
goes after the credibility of the chief witness, the interrogation will be far more threatening and suggestive.
At the very least a kind of nonsensical guilt may form.
"If I hadn't gone to the store at six o'clock, if I lived
in the suburbs this wouldn't have happened to me."

The police work, however sensitive it is, and too
often it is not couched in terms that will keep the
victim tranquil, insinuates a sliver of guilt that will
rankle all but the sturdiest of personalities. Some police also win blue ribbons for male chauvinist piggism.
"Male officers," said a psychiatrist, "often have an
unconscious feeling that women are sexual objects,
should be desired. They come to an investigation feeling that the woman was asking for it." Police bias goes
beyond sexism. A 25-year-old white reporter was forcibly raped by a man who broke into her apartment.
She received high marks for credibility from the cops
until they discovered a poster of Eldrige Cleaver on
her wall during the search for evidence. Their interest

in the case, their belief in her story swiftly drained away. Wrote Dr. Peters, "In the minds of some law enforcement officials, association with blacks is tantamount to asking to be victimized." A white victim who socializes with blacks will find the police less trusting of her allegation of rape. In these instances the victim is made to feel guilty.

Often enough, when gentle support may be most necessary, the victim confronts an incredible piggishness from cops and other agencies. As Martha Eames indicated, a rape victim, to some men, gives off the same heady musk as divorcées once did. Cops do come on with rape victims. What can be expected of men whose commanding officer told a pair of interviewers, "If a woman has a knife at her throat she might as well relax and enjoy it."

The tendency of the policemen to trust the victim sometimes seems directly proportional to the emotional stability of the victim after the rape. The cooler she is in relating her story, the less inclined the cop is to believe her. "I told the policeman what happened. He was distant, seemed skeptical as he took notes, saying nothing to me that would indicate sympathy or concern. Perhaps it was the way I told my story . . . no tears . . . commenting on how skillful the intruder must have been to have climbed into my apartment in the first place. . . . The detective looked at me cooly and said, 'I still don't know exactly what he did do.' And then I realized that he hadn't believed a word."

Credibility is directly proportional to the amount of damage done to the victim. A broken jaw, assorted contusions and lacerations or *summa bonum,* bullet or stab wounds and the victim banks an inexhaustible sum of credibility.

The emotional damage done to the female varies, of course. For forcible rape, as opposed to statutory rape, Philadelphia finds younger females, teen-agers, are more likely to be concerned with the purely sexual aspect of rape. They are the ones who think in terms of becoming contaminated, of becoming unattractive to any respectable boy, the "will anyone ever marry me?" lament. For older women, ones who have been married or who have had sexual experiences, the rape becomes not a sexual act but an aggressive assault upon a sexual area. Mature women, even before the feminist movement, were becoming increasingly assertive of their right to say no, even to a husband. The rapist brutally ignores that right. One researcher theorizes, "Women feel they must yield control, revert to a passive, infantile behavior, a loss of autonomy, something not acceptable to them."

The circumstances surrounding rape may be just as much a shock as the attack itself. "I had a woman who worked for the Board of Education," reported a worker on the Philadelphia study. "She was a kind of retiring person, she had few friends and did not go out often with men. She went to a party with her best friend who arranged a ride home with a man. The guy then raped her and my patient simply retreated to her bed, could not leave the apartment, or work. What demoralized her even more than the rape was the sense that she had been set up by her girl-friend. The one person she had put her faith in, the female figure in whom she needed to believe, betrayed her."

"You find somewhat the same reaction for a woman who is attacked in her apartment or on the street where people are nearby and no one pays any attention to her screams," said Dr. Peters. "That sense of isolation and helplessness can be devastating."

Loss of faith in the male animal is endemic. "They never feel quite the same about men," said a female investigator in Philadelphia. Helen Anne, Kitty Allen and Martha Eames also reported a new wariness toward those of the opposite, potentially threatening, sex. Yvette, like Kitty Allen, found her attitude toward sex complicated. "I suppose what's most disturbing is becoming a thing, an object for use. It's connected with such a beautiful thing. But then it's used to humiliate you."

That the injured parties should be so insecure with men is quite predictable, according to the results of Dr. Peters's studies. "Fear of being raped again has the highest mean score for any type of fear the victim reports. Sixty percent of the sample recorded some fear."

Whether the effects of rape can be differentiated on the basis of race was not discernible. The Philadelphia project believes, tentatively, that class rather than ethnic background figures strongly in the reaction. Middle-class and upper-class people, it is felt, suffer more of an emotional shock because of their lack of familiarity with violence, crime and victimization. The poor, on the other hand, whether black or white, are more accustomed to being oppressed, to casual mayhem. For them, support is more in the nature of guidance toward the right kind of physical services, proper medical treatment to prevent V.D., advice on how to pursue the complaint or how to file for victim's compensation if the state provides such a resource. Even at that, some investigators think that assault is still assault, and that the burden upon the victim's psyche is constant. Said one psychiatrist, "I've talked to girls, black girls who say that you get ripped off by the world every day and rape is just one more rip off. But they may be using that as a means to deny to themselves what happened."

In the main, the families and friends of rape victims have turned out to be surprisingly supportive, at least in the research collected by the Philadelphia project. "In some cases, a good relationship could even be strengthened," said a psychiatrist. However, in those instances where the husband and wife relationship was already troubled before the rape, the crime can be a messy *coup de grace*. A New York City woman's husband simply split the scene after his wife was attacked. In Philadelphia one victim, according to her attending psychiatrist, developed a massive tendency to say no to her husband. For her, the crime had provided an unconscious reinforcement of her desire to say no long enough until her husband would reject her and look elsewhere.

The nuclear family reaches thermonuclear stages with the rape of a child. When a stranger commits rape on a child the problem is much less acute. Everyone can rally to support and express rage at the offender. But when a father or stepfather sexually assaults the youngster, the consequences can include lifelong emotional problems for the victim.

For example, Dr. Peters cited the case of a girl raped at age four-and-a-half. Her father had gone on a business trip and instructed the mother to remain home with the youngster. Instead, the mother took the child to visit with some friends and left her in the custody of the an 18-year-old boy, who raped her. The mother's chief concern appeared to be her own protection, to prevent her husband from learning that she had not supervised their offspring properly. She swore the daughter to secrecy on the grounds that father would be so upset he'd have a heart attack.

The mother's failure to show concern about the assault itself confused the child. She inferred that the kid somehow had been in the wrong. When the victim was 32 she suffered severe sexual anxieties that manifested themselves in a series of phobias designed to keep her housebound. Psychotherapy loosened her behavior slightly, but not enough for her to be able to develop any kind of relationship with a man.

An 11-year-old victim of a babysitter experienced the same maternal reaction, self-protection, not incidentally because her mother had also been having an affair with the culprit. The child was warned that if father learned of the incident, he would murder the offender and get the electric chair. Guilt swamped the child; somehow she had participated in an act that could destroy her father. She became a sleeparound as a young woman. Although in therapy, she was not able to recover until after her father died and she could comfortably unlock the memory of the rape.

When father himself is the guilty party the situation is even more convoluted. Mother is torn between her obligations to her daughter and whatever sentiments she has toward her husband, in spite of his assault. The child is caught in between; the support she expected from her mother is either not forthcoming, or it wavers. The figure she has been taught to respect turns out to be the one who betrays her. "It's enormously complicated," said a Philadelphia psychiatrist. "You get a teasing, angry guy who is the stepfather and a thirteen-year-old girl who is a teasing angry teen-ager. When she tells her mother that the stepfather has assaulted her the mother is torn apart. The guy has been good to her, she does not know whether the kid is fantasizing. Then you get situations where the child keeps silent. It may be a wise decision, in view of the family dynamics."

In Philadelphia a father had assaulted daughters aged 16 and 9. When the girls told their mother, he was indicted, convicted of incest and handed a probationary sentence with the proviso that he undergo psychiatric treatment. He returned home and to his old ways. Mother promptly advised the authorities who withdrew probation. Father went on trial again. The judge served him a 5-to-10-year term. That, in the eyes of mother was too lenient and she appealed for a stiffer sentence. It was trauma upon trauma for the 16-year-old. She had first to cope with the rapes commited by her father, then to endure a second trial in which she appeared not only as the chief witness against her father, but in addition was forced to identify a film that her father made of them during intercourse. Now, her mother, in her hunger for revenge, pushed the child to suffer through still another trial. "Even if it is a stranger," said Dr. Peters, "parents become determined to nail the offender. They don't realize the toll of a trial."

Unfortunately, judicial proceedings, the place where the offender is supposed to get his just desserts, generally traumatizes a victim. At just about the time when she has made her recovery, decided to forget it all, the subpoena arrives, awakening the old fears, forcing her to face her attacker again. Theoretically, as Martha Eames felt, a trial, the defiled's day in court, even the working through of the experience which is often employed by psychiatrists to help patients recover from some stressful moments should be a ca-tharsis. But it doesn't usually work out that way. It's designed to bomb offenders, not as a psychotherapy experience for victims. Unless a woman is in the hands of a sensitive, understanding D.A.—and given the vol-ume of cases, the job tends to squeeze out humanity —she is exposed to a chillingly impersonal world where she finds herself often on trial.

A woman visited the City of Brotherly Love and was rewarded with unbrotherly attentions from three men and a female accomplice. Still in shock from her misadventure she went to the preliminary hearing where she was subject to the first counterpunches of defense. She lost interest in food, could not sleep, quit her job. She tried to beg off from the actual trial but after six months of "intensive support by social and psychiatric staff," including a social worker who at-tended court with her, she managed to make it through ten days of trial before jury. Only two of the accused were found guilty and she remains doubtful whether it was all worthwhile.

Philadelphia's system, which does not differ from most of the urban judicial proceedings, erodes the zeal of most witnesses. Preliminary hearings take place in outlying precincts in atmospheres redolent of the sleazy nature of crime. Defense attorneys seek continuances, delays that require the witness to gear up for an ordeal over and over again, only to find that the torment will not be today, but at some point in the indefinite future. Not surprisingly, witnesses say to hell with it, I want to get back to restoring my life instead of raking up the still searing coals.

As with other elements of rape, some patterns in the victims have been identified by students of the phenomenon. The Institute for Sex Research, working over the histories of sex offenders sketched a composite of victims as averaging 24 years of age, with a goodly chunk under 20. "Older women were definitely more immune to rape: only 3 percent of the victims were 51 or over." It's like the narcotics epidemic: If you live past a certain age you don't seem to catch it.

Amir, working over the Philadelphia data on victims, put the peak age slightly lower but he too found that in advanced age there is safety. Does it mean that the rapist concerns himself with traditional values of the sexual object, youth, beauty? Does it mean that the rapist generally associates with women his age and therefore the choice of victims is explained? In those instances where an older woman is attacked, could the offender be acting out the Oedipus scene? Nobody has been able to formulate any factual answers to these questions.

"It wasn't rape—she took her clothes off," protested a number of offenders screened by the Institute for Sex Research. That the woman had just been threatened with severe physical pain or even death, or that she might have been automatonized through fear had been blocked out by these attackers. The defense is the extreme end of the entire notion of what has been variously named as "provoked rape," "victim-precipitated rape" and "assumption of risk." But the word rape, legally and by the grace of Noah Webster as well, cancels out the exculpatory adjectives except, perhaps, as mitigating any sentence from a judge.

Victim-precipitated rape was summed up in the *Washington Post* by Coleman McCarthy, "The theory is that the male interpreted the woman's behavior as a direct invitation for sex. The woman who invites her dates 'up for a drink' or accepts a ride with a male friend is thus seen as teasing; she is not raped but seduced—in the grand manner of Casanova, or Marlon Brando doing his tango in Paris. Victim-precipitated rape is the equivalent of victim-precipitated robbery; bank tellers shouldn't have so much money just over the window, it only teases the people to rob it." McCarthy's unfortunate analogy with the bank, the public site, the robbery by the stranger confuses the notion of victim-precipitated rape. A palpable object has been stolen. There is no potential element of pleasure for the bank or its employee.

The subject came up during a meeting in Philadelphia of the Center for Rape Concern. A staff member spoke of a case in which a woman met a man at a bar and after an evening of conviviality he offered to drive her home. On the way he said he would have to stop at his motel to pick up something. At the place he invited her to his room and subsequently she cried rape. One psychiatrist called this a perfect example of victim-precipitated rape; another would only call it an instance of poor judgment. A social scientist postulated, "Suppose he had stolen her purse, would that have been listed as victim precipitated?" In the absence of any brutality toward the victim, the issue would become, which party does one believe on the question of consent. If the villain had taken her purse the defense might easily be the same. "I asked her would she lend me fifty bucks and she said sure and then I guess when she thought about it she changed her mind." Given the mentality of some cops, they might be less likely to believe that a woman would lend her money than her body, even to a relative stranger. (There have been a disagreeable number of calls for the cops to pick up someone for car theft when in reality the owner had, after lending the vehicle, for one reason or another, felt aggrieved enough to injure the former friend.)

Still, few juries, if the case were to go that far, would take the stance that because the woman went to the man's motel room that made her an accomplice to the theft of her valuables. But when it comes to a less tangible valuable, we the materialistic refuse to believe.

Amir noted what he called "victim precipitation" in the dynamics of rape. He defines it as "situations in which the victim actually, or so it was deemed, agreed to sexual relations but retracted before the actual act or did not react strongly enough when the suggestion was made by the offender." Amir also included "risky situations marred with sexuality, especially when she uses what could be interpreted as indecency in language and gestures, or [does something that] constitutes what could be taken as an invitation to sexual relations."

He relied on the fact that nearly 20 percent of the victims had police records, mostly for sexual offenses, that another 20 percent had sexually enticing reputations and a significant number of crimes began with victim meeting perpetrator in an atmosphere that eroded the normal restrictions on behavior.

The "victim did it" concept threads its way through the minds of even some of the allegedly more enlightened. The criminal courts judge, talking to a community meeting in New York about the difficulties in court proceedings against rapists who said, "Let's face it. If you wear a short skirt, if you sit with your legs apart, you do arouse feelings in a man," reflects a bias against the victim. The psychiatrist who spoke of one of his patients suffering from a rape-induced emotional upset—"she invited it by hitchhiking at four o'clock in the morning"—obscures the line between his idea of prudent behavior and the rights of another human living under a code that forbids rape.

According to Eric Berne, "Rapo" is one of the games people play. "Third Degree Rape is a vicious game which ends in murder, suicide or the courtroom. Here White leads Black into compromising physical contact and then claims that he has made a criminal assault or has done her irreparable damage. In its most cynical form, White may actually allow him to complete the sexual act so that she gets that enjoyment before confronting him. The confrontation may be immediate, as in the illegitimate cry of rape. . . ."

It would seem that without a scorecard one will have difficulty in determining who did what unto whom. Mushing the line between right and wrong, between truth and untruth, between victim and offender is something of a national pastime.

VII

Something of the Nature of the Beast

If material on victims is something less than solid, that on the offenders is downright gossamer. Rapists do not often come under the discriminating eyes of behavioral scientists. For openers, rapists are not readily identified in the population. Those accused of sex offenses, because of the generally acknowledged difficulty of obtaining convictions for the crime, because of the opprobrium heaped upon them in prisons, go behind the big walls for crimes other than rape. Without rape on the record, the criminologists and psychologists studying prison populations may not be aware of the individual with whom they are dealing. Those who are identified as rapists are generally not permitted into the kind of situations where the behavioral scientists can study them. Researchers know from experience that the rapist is seldom released to a halfway house or a prerelease program.

"They will take anyone except the rapist. They do not want people who possibly have psychological problems," said one investigator. "Second, most communities are unhappy about a halfway house in their midst and one concession to the community is to keep out convicted rapists." Finally, rapists as a group, show great reluctance to cooperate in therapy and research. Some, for the reason that they do not feel they committed a crime [she asked for it], and others because they do not wish to admit publicly to a sex crime.

Ignorance gives birth to all species of theory that can masquerade as truth until the vacuum of ignorance is filled. A modest start at filling the void is in *Sex Offenders*, the 1965 tome containing findings by the Institute for Sex Research. One chapter deals with 140 "heterosexual aggressors vs. adults" which was the closest classification to include rapists. It admittedly covers those males guilty of forced sodomy as well. Institute surveys show the rapist on the lower end of the scale when it comes to "good adjustment with either father or mother." In addition, more aggressors versus adults got along better with their mothers than with their fathers. A psychoanalytic configuration for the rapist postulates a seductive but rejecting maternal figure. About 60 percent of the offenders come from broken homes. In their psychic tree appears one prominent branch, an unusual tendency to fantasize with a distinct orientation toward sadomasochistic daydreams. One could call it an omen of things to come, but more likely wishing makes it horribly real.

As adolescents the heterosexual aggressors experienced a considerable amount of sexual experiences, including a high amount of premarital coitus. Almost 60 percent of them married (not necessarily by the time of their offense), however, and it was predicted that three-quarters of them would wed by the time they reached age 35. One other significant aspect of their marital history was a tendency to marry more than once. Of all of the sex offenders, the heterosexual aggressors versus adults showed the greatest frequency of marital coitus, which should destroy any notion that rapists lack sexual contact. In addition, the heterosexual aggressors group was into a heavy variety of sexual experiences, anal coitus, a high proportion of oral-genital acts. "This is not unexpected in a group which was little troubled by moral restraints and had a strong proclivity toward taboo sexual techniques," said *Sex Offenders*. Interestingly, the wives of these offenders did not enjoy their spouses' attentions greatly. "A moderate number reached orgasm regularly, but nearly one-fifth of their married years were marred by low (less than 10 percent) orgasm rates." In addition the Institute for Sex Research remarked that the high incidence of anal coitus, presumed to be painful and humiliating to the female, indicated a potentially sadistic streak in the men. Additionally, members of the group exhibited a high degree of sexual arousal from pictures or stories with sadomasochistic material.

Fidelity was not one of their strong points; 77 percent were unfaithful. Except for time they spent in prison, the heterosexual aggressors dabbled in homosexuality no more than the average American male.

"As for how they evaluated the happiness of their marriages the aggressors are in no way unusual; their marriages were not especially happy or unhappy in comparison to those of the other groups" (which included normal individuals).

Perhaps most revealing about the heterosexual aggressors was the extremely high percentage of them (87 percent) that had been convicted of some sort of crime by age 25. Many of these were serious offenses, ones that had put them in a penitentiary for a minimum of one year. Half of the convictions were for sex crimes.

The previous sex crimes convictions were those against "willing or acquiescent females" (statutory rape, consensual sodomy or exhibition and peeping). The exhibitionism has been interpreted by Dr. Peters as a natural precursor to rape. "They have a desire to shock or offend women and start by exhibitionism. But that's not shocking anymore, so they go on to direct assault." Many of the heterosexual aggressors were convicted on peeping charges, but that was not to be interpreted as a characteristic of the timid voyeur. Instead, it was the first step toward the crime, surveillance that allows proper selection of victim, time, place, method of entry and so on.

The group that includes rapists displayed a consistent disregard for other prohibitions and the men were arrested for a variety of antisocial activities, marked by one predilection, offenses against other humans, rather than those involving public order or property.

At the time of the offense which brought them to the

attention of the Institute (or, more correctly, first to the police) the aggressors averaged just under 25. Between one-quarter and one-third were married, another quarter separated, divorced or widowed, the remainder unmarried. Previous to the crime, about 5 percent had demonstrated enough troubles to have been either institutionalized or labeled neurotic. When they attacked, 39 percent were determined to be drunk, another 15 percent only mildly intoxicated. Drugs other than alcohol proved to be insignificant in their presence.

Some, but not all of the qualities of the rapist as seen by the Institute for Sex Research were confirmed by Menachem Amir in Philadelphia. His research discovered the majority of offenders to be between the ages of 15–24, with the peak between 15 and 19. Only 16 percent of the 1292 rapists studied by Amir were married, less than 1 percent separated or divorced. Because Amir went at his work as a criminologist, he did not bring to bear the same criteria as did the Institute for Sex Research. Unfortunately he does not have anything to offer on the psychiatric profiles of the rapists. He does report a correlation between alcohol and rape; but he also finds whiskey, wine or beer present in both victim and perpetrator was the most common circumstance in which alcohol was on the scene. Amir breaks down his data on alcohol and other matters by race (more white rapists got up their courage via booze than black ones) but that only emphasizes a major weakness of Amir's work. He is dependent upon the police for the information. Philadelphia cops, in 1958 and 1960, like most big city police, were highly insensitive to blacks and their troubles. Determinations that one or both parties had been drinking therefore hinges only on some cop's word; it may not have been considered relevant by another policeman and left off the sheet. How loaded one or both parties were is a subjective determination. When you spice the judgment with racial prejudice, the data seems even less reliable.

The role of alcohol in crimes has perplexed investigators. One school insists that alcohol excites sexual desire. Another holds that the place where whiskey is dispensed establishes an ambience that leads to a relationship. The Israeli criminologist is sophisticated enough to note the inconsistencies in various studies of the rape-and-alcohol cocktail. He cites reports that found alcohol in rape situations as high as 75 percent and as low as zero. The last, unfortunately, is a California compilation in 1930–1932. Amir appears ignorant that the "Noble Experiment" (Prohibition) still was parching American throats at the time. Whatever else it may be, alcohol figures as one of the great copouts in rape. "I musta been drunk," is part of the policeman's version of *Bartlett's Familiar Quotations*.

When he searched the Philadelphia police files, and those of the FBI, for information on the previous records of the 1292 rapists, Amir confirmed the Institute for Sex Research in its configuration of the rapist as no stranger to the cops. A fraction less than half had been booked at some time in their lives. "The persistency of violating the law is noted here," remarked Amir. The Israeli parted company with the Institute on the nature of the criminal acts other than the sex offense.

About a third of the records indicated offenses against people, the rest centered on crimes against property, rupture of public order; there was also a small number of drug arrests.

Among the more widely held theses concerning sex criminals is that they are so driven that when released from prison they go right back to their old antisocial habits. Amir reviewed the meager literature on the rate of recidivism for rapists and sex offenders. He came up with the qualified conclusion that the odds on rapists repeating their sin after once being caught is low. His caveat is grounded on the scrappiness of the information available. Students of the U.S. rapist are further put off by the amount of dependence upon foreign investigations, and domestic studies that are 30–40 years old.

A New York City mayor's committee in 1940 flatly concluded that rapists are not abnormal persons, nor are their crimes abnormalities but only an offshoot of their criminal propensities. Rape, said the committee, is frequently just incidental, committed with another type of crime, or because of the influence of alcohol, or as a gang activity, which "more than once brought them into conflict with the law for other than sexual offenses." The data for this determination came apparently from offenders traced backward from 1939 to 1930.

When Pennsylvania began to study the history of rapists, the participating social scientists decided "the only rate of recidivism lower than that for sex offenses is the rate for criminal homicide." Amir called a foot fault on that leap to a conclusion. The Pennsylvania findings depended upon a look at 523 rapists without regard to the disposition of their cases. Those who were convicted of the crime and did time, turned out to have a depressingly repetitive pattern.

Other sources that diminish the bogey man sex fiend are European in their origins. They may involve offenders of quite a different psychic stripe. London, the site of one of the studies, currently reports perhaps one-tenth the number of rapes that New York does, although the population figures are relatively close. As in everything, there may be a point where quantitative difference also implies a qualitative one.

What is surprising is that these investigations, for all of their failings, are the only ones that have focused on the histories of sex criminals. And still, in spite of a lack of contradictory material, they failed as a contraceptive to that popular chimera, the stop-me-before-I-rape-again fellow.

The Institute for Sex Research divided its aggressors versus adults into seven varieties. The most common type, somewhere between one-quarter and one-third of the entire group, were labeled the "assaultive variety." For these individuals, sexual activity alone did not satisfy; actual physical violence or the serious threat of it added a necessary ingredient to their diet. "They generally do not know their victim; they usually commit the offense alone, without accomplices . . . the use of weapons is common; the man usually has a past history of violence . . . [there] is a tendency for the offense to be accompanied by bizarre behavior including unnecessary and trivial theft."

The text offers several cases. Rather than further

debase the Institute's example with the anonymity of "a man," I will call him Charlie. Since puberty, Charlie had gotten his jollies from tales of rape and he improvised his own fantasy of breaking into a house at night and there tearing off a girl's clothes. She then became so aroused that she turned most cooperative. At age 15, while peeping, he attempted to put this scenario into production, crashing into a home where he had watched a woman undress. He had altered his script slightly. Instead of counting upon her willing surrender, he bashed her on the head with the handle of a knife to render her unconscious and vulnerable for coitus. But maybe Charlie had seen too many films where a single thump on the head brings unconsciousness (the skull is very hard, a fact to which any boxer who has hit someone on the top of the head with his fist will attest). The blow delivered by Charlie only caused the woman to screech for help and he fled.

Seven years later, Charlie, banking on a rumor of her promiscuity, charged into the home of a neighboring woman at night. According to his version, he found her asleep, awakened her, put his hand over her mouth and warned her to be quiet and then began to caress her. He told investigators that she responded with enthusiasm, so much so that she invited him to return the following evening. Unfortunately for Charlie, she went to the cops after he left and Charlie was arrested. However, the neighbor took pity on Charlie since she was a friend of his mother and refused to press charges. Charlie was released with advice to seek psychiatric help.

Charlie married a year later, but the nuptial bed

lacked that necessary ingredient for his sex life. Twice he seized women outdoors at night but their screams scared him off. He made two night house calls but quickly departed upon the discovery that the male member of the family was at home. Charlie's marriage broke up and he pursued rape more earnestly, failing in all instances because of screams or subterfuges by the victim. On his final try he succumbed again to the suggestion that he call again when she was not menstruating. When he made his second appearance, the police were on hand. The Charlies of the world come closest to the compulsive rapist, the man who cannot satisfy himself without at least a soupçon of the old SM.

The second most common type of aggressors were the "amoral" men. "They were not sadistic—they simply wanted to have coitus and the females' wishes are of no particular consequence. They are not hostile toward females, but look upon them solely as sexual objects whose role in life is to provide sexual pleasure." It is a description that many feminists believe would fit most men, except that a substantial number aren't willing to break the law in order to enjoy themselves.

Almost as frequent were the alcoholically inspired aggressors. "The drunk's aggression ranges from uncoordinated grapplings and pawings, which he construes as efforts at seduction, to hostile and truly vicious behavior released by intoxication." That's all neatly put but since there's no evidence of whiskey as an aphrodisiac the category appears artificial. The question remains, why, when under the influence, did these men resort to force?

About 10 to 15 percent of the aggressors versus adults were termed "the explosive variety." They were akin to individuals who suffered "traumatic neurosis," a reaction to some sudden stress. Loss of job, serious illness in the family preceded the crime. Physical violence was the means to overcome resistance, rather than the end itself.

Closely akin to the amoral crowd were the "double-standard" offenders. They separated females into good girls and bad ones. Women who allowed themselves to be picked up in bars or similar circumstances (remember that this research began covering offenders before 1965) appeared to be legitimate prey. But unlike their amoral counterparts, the double-standard operators made an attempt to persuade or seduce before going to the heavier stuff. The other point of difference with the amorals was that some females, the ones the rapists expected to marry or their sisters, they rated as untouchables.

The Institute lumped the remainder of offenders into either mental defectives and psychotics or mixtures of various groupings. It's not a terribly scientific approach, but it does offer some classification and taken in conjunction with Amir's work, the research serves as a foundation for further probing.

Because they operate one of the few ongoing projects dealing with sex offenders, the Philadelphia Rape Concern Program meets a steady demand for stories from the media and information that will enable cities to better protect their citizenry. Commonly, everyone wants to know who is the most dangerous and how can you detect him. "We always say that the most dangerous offender is one who will force himself upon you," said Dr. Peters, "whether he is just an exhibitionist, a homosexual or a rapist. It is not the form of the offense, it is the zeal with which the man pursues it."

On the other hand, Dr. Peters is willing to generalize on the background of the dangerous offender. That includes the rapist, although the Philadelphia program deals mainly with first offenders who have not been handed long prison sentences. Except for a few probationers who committed forcible rape, the treatment population so far as rape is concerned consists mainly of the statutory variety. "The dangerous offender," said Dr. Peters, "has probably been beaten as a child, saw his father beat women. He has decided that this is the way men treat women. He has a record of antisocial behavior across the board," a judgment proclaimed also by the Institute for Sex Research and Amir.

"He has a record," continued Dr. Peters, "but not usually for violent crimes, more likely to do with interpretation of the rules of the game. Instead of their being without conscience, many are extremely afraid of authority, could be from a strict religious fundamentalism." Not coincidentally, two recently arrested rapists who prowled Manhattan were the sons of ministers.

"Relationships at home generally have fallen apart, there's a generous intake of alcohol. You have to be careful about that question of a police record, however. Almost every black in a community like down-town Philadelphia has a record. We had expected these fellows to be impulse ridden. Instead they came up a somewhat low ego and a very high overactive superego, the model for Freud's vision of psy-choneurosis. During the Victorian Age with rigid so-cial rules, a superego like that made a person a neu-rotic. Today, with the social rules shifting, you get antisocial behavior. We seem to see more and more of the sociopaths or character disorders. They don't suffer anxiety, like the neurotic but they commit a lot of antisocial acts. And what happens when the kid finds that if he exhibits himself it doesn't shock the woman. He must do something more than visual, something really assaultive." ["Attention must be paid," cried Arthur Miller's moribund salesman, Wil-lie Loman. He was willing to accept a modest token of recognition. The rapist assesses heavier dues.]

"I don't buy the thesis of a subculture of violence that breeds rape," said Dr. Peters, thereby exposing one of the running sores of rapeology. The subculture explanation, held by sociologist Marvin E. Wolfgang who serves on the Center for Studies in Sexual Devi-ance, and by Menachem Amir rejects psycholanalytic theories on the forces that generate rape. Sociologists tend to dismiss claims that the fault lies in an in-dividual's manhandling of sexual libido, aggression, suppression, sublimation, guilt. In psychoanalytic terms it's all in his mind and the penis forced into the unwilling vagina resolves the problem temporarily. *The Awarding of the Penis as a Compensation for Rape*; *Psychopathology of Sexual Delinquency*; *A Fetish Theory of*

Amorous Fixation; these are typical routes explored in scientific papers along the psychiatric frontier. Those who incline to the psychoanalytic approach opt for an inductive approach; the case of a Charlie maps out a whole territory of rapists. However, sociologists and criminologists prefer the deductive approach, piling up and sifting data and looking at the problem as a socially derived one. Amir and others like him contend that an individual within a group (i.e., the black in the ghetto) may deviate from the mores of the larger society if his subculture tolerates or condones types of sexual behavior ordinarily condemned. The argument is that the black ghetto accepts a subculture of violence conducive to forcible rape which explains why the incidence of the crime is higher among nonwhites. Even sociologists who disagree with Amir's racial connotation will accept the proposition that rape sprouts more readily among all the poor presumably because, as one approaches the base line of subsistence, the violence level in relationships rises.

Less doubt surrounds the ugliest form of rape, pedophilia. It takes a Charles Manson type of subculture to condone assaults upon children. What appalls the public in pedophilia, however, is less the use of force than the object of the attentions. On a lesser scale Vladimir Nabokov scandalized a portion of America with *Lolita*, a story that centered on a middle-aged man's affair with a prepubescent girl. (Henry Luce resisted publication of a profile on Nabokov because he considered *Lolita* dirty, although the author was writing about everything other than pedophilia.)

Still, the pedophiliac is one of the toughest to bring

to justice. "The greatest rate of nonpreferred charges," is the experience of Dr. Peters. It should be distinguished from the greatest rate of unfoundeds, which applies to alleged rapes against adolescents. Part of the problem is the reluctance of the family to pursue the matter since the offender is often a member of the family or a friend. The second obstacle is the problem of evidence. A child under a certain age may not be sworn in as a witness and it is the right of a judge to determine whether the child can be considered competent. When one adds to that the requirement that sodomy (often the form of pedophilia) requires corroborative material, the chances of making it stick became minimal. Detective Tom Kelly in the Bronx said, "There's this Irishman, a retired city employee, he's been arrested five times for sodomizing kids and in three different boroughs of the city. I visited the house where he lived, knocked on the door, a woman opened up downstairs and when I said I was a detective, I wanted to see the fellow who lived above, she answered, 'Oh, you mean the sex criminal. It's time you did something about him.' Another neighbor also called him a 'sex nut.' But he knows the law and he denies everything. He says the kids come to him, give him a hard luck story and so he lends them money. Then when the mother can't pay it back she accuses him of sodomy. No way, this has happened in three different boroughs with five different mothers. The D.A. talked to him for two-and-a-half hours but couldn't get him to even talk to a psychiatrist. There's nothing we can do about him, and everybody in the neighborhood seems to be on to him."

How to rewrite the laws on this type of case and still protect against the malicious or warped child has, so far, defied reason.

Amir included in his study paragraphs about "sexual humiliation," which might be taken to be another form of violence beyond the need to intimidate the victim. Fellatio, cunnilingus, the anal approach, use of a prophylactic (because, said Amir, in some rather tortured logic, it indicated that the rapist considered himself engaged in a relationship of genuine affection or else sought to protect himself against disease) and repeated intercourse were classified as sexually humiliating. These versions of sexual humiliation presented themselves in slightly more than 25 percent of the rapes in 1958 and 1960. Based on the evidence, starting with the first Kinsey report, which suggested that oral to genital sexual expression is increasingly popular for both sexes in the United States, the notion that these forms qualify as sexual humiliation seems anachronistic. The standard missionary position, male superior to the female, could be interpreted as sexual humiliation by a woman. And in fact the real humiliation of rape is that one party has forced his attentions on another.

A policewoman like Lieutenant Julia Tucker, concerned with crime prevention and apprehension of rapists divides offenders into two groups; "the opportunist and the pathological. No matter what you do, the pathological rapist gets his kicks by violently attacking women."

Some offenders just don't fit that easily. Is the night-crawling burglar who discovers a woman in the house an opportunist or did he intend all along to commit an assault? Into what category would one slide Eldridge Cleaver during his brief rape career? Lots of men find themselves in the position of the so-called opportunist. What keeps them from forcible rape? Dr. Peters professes to believe in a psychiatric explanation; yet he accepts the notion that the social situation manipulates the form of expression for hang-ups. Menachem Amir chooses the subculture of violence, but overlooks the fact that the existence of such a subculture can never explain why only *certain individuals within the subculture* resort to rape.

Underlying all theories is the nature of man. Are all men potential rapists? Circumstances do make a difference. Conquering armies embark on rapine as a matter of course, often without any serious effort to control the abuse. In itself, this implies that rape is abnormal behavior, actions suited to abnormal times and permitted as a punishment to the enemy and a reward to men deprived of sexual release. But circumstances are only part of the equation.

Once social scientists automatically lumped the rapist among the pathological specimens of humanity. But a persistent current of contemporary thought continues to see the rapist as the average man. Susan Griffin in *Ramparts* quoted a parole officer from the prison at San Luis Obispo: "These men [rapists] were the most normal men there. They had a lot of hang-ups, but they were the same hang-ups as men walking out on the street."

Then Ms. Griffin cited Menachem Amir: "Studies indicate that sex offenders do not constitute a unique or psychopathological type nor are they as a group more disturbed than the control groups to which they were compared." Fine and good, for Amir continues, "As for his personality profile, he was found to have a normal personality and normal sexual instincts as measured by his choice of victim for sexual gratification." Then Amir opens up a little mushroom cloud. "However, almost all of the studies show that he has a pronounced tendency to be impulsive, aggressive and violent." That nice normal chap with common hang-ups who happens to commit rape was given to outbursts of mayhem that took the form of a sexual assault. Amir's definition of normal, and the one accepted by Ms. Griffin thus encompasses all but the gibbering psychotic.

No lawyer has yet attempted to plead a rape client not guilty on the grounds of an uncontrollable sexual urge. On the other hand, to conclude that the rapist is an ordinary man who finds himself in a certain place, at a certain time, under certain external influences is to defy the statistical evidence on rape. The very circumstances under which the majority of rapes occur—a date, a pickup, a party, a boy-friend's visit, a couple of alcoholic drinks, a flirtation—are human transactions that occur millions of times daily. Only a minute fraction terminate in a rape. The question of the chemistry involved has not yet been answered.

VIII

Trial by Trial

The courtroom is where all of the differing cell-like
particles of a sexual happening come together to be
judged as a rape or some other social phenomenon.
Accused and accuser confront one another. Expert
conflicts with expert. The law comes forward: that
which is engraved on statute books, that which is en-
crusted in the time-bound precedents of case law. The
attorneys, those for the state, those for the defendant,
surrogate adversaries in logic and prejudice for jury
and judge, do combat.

Criminal law is not supposed to be trial by ordeal,
but sometimes it works out that way. Criminal law is
not supposed to be *mano a mano*, but the *State* v. *John
Doe*. Yet, in a rape action, the very nature of the
offense makes the issue come down to a case of her
word against his more often than in any other crime.
Criminal proceedings are not supposed to be

weighted to the advantage of any group by reason of race, creed, color or sex. The aim is to protect the rights of the individual accused, but in a rape case the accused is always a man, the accuser a woman. Not designed that way, the protection extended to the defendant, a man, puts the onus on the chief witness, the woman.

About 4 P.M. on a Sunday afternoon in July, Ellen Browning, a white, Mississippi-born, 24-year-old part-time student at Columbia University, a former VISTA worker, the separated wife of Alfred Browning, and at the moment a peddler of flowers, left her Upper West Side apartment in Manhattan to stroll to the tennis courts along the banks of the Hudson River where she thought she might see her close friend Jeffrey Wolf.

He was not there, however, and Ellen Browning sat down on a park bench to savor the late afternoon sun and read J. P. Donleavy's *Short Stories.* After a short time, she was approached by a slim black man, George Elliot. He offered some casual conversation, sat down beside her, talked a bit about the book—he was unfamiliar with J. P. Donleavy—and remarked that he was a construction worker who had come to the park for a political rally.

Some 20 minutes after the opening of this conversation, Ellen Browning announced that she had an appointment with a friend for the evening and began to walk back toward her apartment. She offered no objection when Elliot asked to accompany her during the trip. En route, Ellen stopped at a phone booth to call her friend, Wolf, but she received no answer.

Instead of going on home, she stopped in at the

West End, a cafe on Broadway in the shadow of Columbia University. Elliot stayed with her while she had several beers, bought a hamburger and Coke and even spoke to some acquaintances. She telephoned Wolf two more times but he was still away. During the talk that passed, Elliot suggested they pick up some groceries, then retire to her apartment and she could prepare dinner. She replied that that was out of the question.

At 9 P.M. Ellen Browning told Elliot that she was heading for home. He paid for both his and her beer and offered to escort her home. She accepted. To this point, there was little dispute about the events themselves. Interpretation, of course, differed greatly when the matter reached the courts.

Ellen Browning's account of what followed became the basis for a rape trial. At the entrance to her building, she said, Elliot asked if he could come up and she refused him. He asked if he could at least use the bathroom. She hesitated, then agreed.

A small elevator carried the pair to the sixth floor where she lived. After she unlocked the door, she told Elliot that as soon as he finished he could simply leave through the open front door. Meanwhile, she went to the kitchen for a soft drink. From there she noticed that Elliot had not closed the bathroom door while he urinated. That alarmed her enough to attempt to leave the apartment.

Elliot grabbed her, clapped one hand over her mouth and dragged her to the bedroom. He pushed her down on the bed and ordered her to remove her clothes. She begged off, asked to be allowed to get a drink. Elliot held her by the arm as she walked to the kitchen, poured herself a glass of Pepsi-Cola. She walked toward the kitchen window but Elliot yanked her away, causing some of the soda to spill. On the trip back to the bedroom, the young woman tossed the glass full of Pepsi into Elliot's face; it splashed on him, soaked her shirt and the wall. She threw the emptied glass to the floor where it shattered. She hoped, said Ellen Browning to take some shards for a weapon.

Elliot dragged her inside the bedroom, shoved her against the wall, put his hands about her neck and began to squeeze. He told Ellen Browning that if she "didn't calm down, he would get violent." She freed herself long enough to try to push out a bedroom screen but it was nailed to the window. When Elliot advanced again she lifted a nearby bathroom scale as a weapon, but he snatched it away.

Down on the bed she went, told again to take off her clothes. She complained that she was having her period; to prove it she pulled her jeans down, lowering her panties enough for him to see a sanitary napkin, some stains on it. Elliot dismissed the condition as an excuse. He forced her to undress, stripped away his garments and mounted her. Although she resisted, Elliot penetrated Ellen Browning's vagina. She pleaded that she was too tense and could they pause for a discussion. Elliot withdrew momentarily, but then pushed her legs apart and commenced anew. For a second time, she succeeded in talking him into a temporary halt. From under a bedcover, Mississipian, Vista worker, Ellen Browning questioned her attacker about his motivation, "whether it was a racial matter."

He offered no reply, only returned to the task of her ravishment. He pinned her hands behind her back. "At this point, I just sort of blocked everything out," said Ellen Browning. After Elliot dressed and left, Ellen Browning recovered, tore off her soda drenched shirt and then donned clean clothes. This time when she called Jeffrey Wolf he answered. Within a few minutes he arrived at her place. In the interval between the telephone call, and Wolf's appearance, Ellen Browning discovered on the floor by the bed a wallet with 16 identification cards, papers and photographs, all belonging to Elliot.

Wolf, a recent law-school graduate, drew from the young woman an account of her ordeal and then telephoned the police. The time was now about 11 P.M. Elliot had been gone for an hour. Patrolman Howard J. Hertel and his partner Patrolman John Spink responded to a radio signal to investigate a rape complaint, arriving at the apartment ten minutes after Wolf's call. The cops noticed the sobbing woman, reported that she showed some nervousness when questioned. Hertel saw liquid (the soda) "running all over the wall." To Spink she said she had been raped and he observed the broken glass on the floor as well as the wet smears on the wall and floor.

Detective Leo Suarez was next to appear on the scene in answer to the report from the patrolmen to the precinct. He too noticed Mrs. Browning's near hysteria and, in addition, spotted an inch-long bruise on the left side of her neck. She told Suarez that she had been raped. Outcry to the police has not generally been accepted in legal doctrine as material that supports a finding of rape, but delay or failure to do so mitigates against a prosecutrix. However, a complaint to a third party not connected with the police, such as Jeffrey Wolf, in some trials has been accepted as tending to support the charge of rape.

Suarez, after taking possession of the wallet and papers that belonged to Elliot, drove Ellen Browning to St. Luke's hospital. Dr. Jagdish Chandra Wadhwa, a specialist in obstetrics and gynecology examined the victim. He noted the bruise on the left side of her neck as well as another on her buttocks. His microscopic view of samples drawn from the young woman's vagina revealed active sperm, proof of recent sexual intercourse.

With the chief witness taken care of, Detective Suarez and a fellow officer went to the address they found in Elliot's wallet. A few hours before dawn they arrested him on the charge of rape. The alleged crime had occured while New York State laws demanded that all three elements in a rape case, penetration, force or lack of consent, and identity, be corroborated. On the basis of the police reports and Ellen Browning's word, a D.A. was able to secure an indictment against Elliot.

For almost two years the accused, unable to make bail, stayed in prison waiting for his trial. Coupled with the normal delays caused by choked court calendars, was Elliot's inability to agree with Legal Aid Society lawyers on how his defense should be handled.

After the jury selection, the judge's remarks to the jury on proper behavior for them and some preliminary sparring between the opposing counsels, the district attorney delivered his opening statement. After recounting the steps that led Elliot to Ellen Browning's apartment, the prosecutor picked up the tempo: "He grabbed her by the ankles and he pulled her lower down on the bed. She was talking and she was trying to get him out. He didn't respond. She pulled her head away. He tried to kiss her and she pulled her head away. He stopped and told her to open her legs. She refused. He put great pressure on her thighs, below the hips, opened up her legs, spread her legs apart. She was under pain. . . . He took her palms, her hands, placed them behind her under the small of her back, making her immobile. Then he penetrated her vagina with his penis." The language did more than tell what happened. It was a dramatization designed to make the jury empathize, feel the terror and the violence.

Defense opened cooly. "Now they spent, we will concede, approximately four hours together talking with each other and drinking beer. And thereafter we will concede that the two of them left the West End Bar . . . entered the building together, went to the top floor in the elevator . . . we will concede that he had intercourse with Mrs. Browning. We will not concede that this intercourse was not with her permission, was the result of force."

Guided by the district attorney, Ellen Browning detailed her background and what had happened that afternoon and evening as she remembered it. Worked into the record was her size, 5′2″, 102 pounds, which would be compared with the 5′9″, 160 pounds of the defendant. From Ellen Browning, the prosecutor drew answers that indicated the conversation on the park bench had been a desultory one; Elliot did not know anything about literature and while he was voluble enough about his family and his career, she responded only "because I felt sorry for him." She said she had not invited him to accompany her when she left the park, but that he tagged along and she was again unwilling to flatly reject him.

Witness Browning intimated she had some unease about his continued attention at the West End cafe where she not only called Jeffrey Wolf several times but looked unsuccessfully for some close friends to join them. The possibility that a kind of contractual relationship had developed between the pair with Elliot's payment for the beers was countered by her answer, "I was going to pay for my drinks and instead he paid for them, and offered to walk me home. And I considered it, you know, a gentlemanly gesture."

At this moment in the trial, Ellen Browning appeared to lose some composure. She requested and was granted a five minute recess.

The examination by the prosecutor continued when the court reconvened. As he led her through the happenings in her apartment, he attempted to defuse potential land mines that might be exploded by the defense. No, she had not screamed because she was never able to get close enough to an open window where she might be heard. As a testament to her resistance, she offered her smashed glass tumbler and her hope to use a piece on Elliot. She did lower her jeans, but only to convince her attacker that this was an inappropriate time of the month for her to have intercourse. She could not remember if in the final assault she had taken off her clothes under duress or Elliot had stripped them away.

In every rape trial, the act itself must be fully entered upon the record: "When you say he was in you, what do you mean?"

"Oh, well, well his penis was in my vagina."

Having established by her word that penetration had occurred, the prosecutor turned to the issue of force.

"When he tried to kiss you, did you consent?"

"No."

"When he grabbed you after he came out of the bathroom, did *you* consent?"

"No."

"After you got the Pepsi-Cola and threw it at him, did you consent to sexual intercourse?"

"No."

"After he tried to strangle you and put you on the bed, did you consent?"

"No."

There was no real need for additional evidence to confirm the identity of the alleged perpetrator. In the defense's opening statement, it had been admitted that the accused had had sexual intercourse with Ellen Browning on the night in question. Nevertheless, the wallet with the papers that belonged to Elliot was made an evidential exhibit to explain how Elliot came to be arrested and charged.

The cross-examination by the defense began. Inconsequential requests for information about the clothes she wore on that day were followed by a sharper line of attack on her relationships. Having told the court that she had been separated from her husband of two years at the time of the crime, Ellen Browning said, "I had a roommate for a while. I also lived with the person I'm living with, the person I'm living with now, a man. For a while, I lived alone, I was living alone that summer."

Asked what made up the conversation between her and Elliot, she replied, "We had very little in common. I thought we came from a very different class, that he'd been culturally deprived, and that indeed we did not have very much in common."

"What was your relationship with Jeffrey Wolf?"

"Our relationship was intimate."

"Is it true, Miss Browning, that you and Mr. Elliot went back from the West End Bar and Grill, back to that apartment, your apartment for that purpose [sexual intercourse]?

"No."

"Your former husband, was he white or black?"

"White."

Defense wondered about her failure to show any alarm as Elliot accompanied her home. It openly pondered why Ellen Browning did not yell for the police at any time; she lived in the immediate neighborhood of Frank Hogan, then the chief district attorney for Manhattan and a man whose home was always guarded by policemen. The witness professed to be totally unaware of Hogan's residence.

The cross-examiner interjected, "Isn't the real truth that you returned to your apartment for sexual intercourse?"

"No."

When Jeffrey Wolf took the stand he had little to offer beyond a straightforward report of the telephone call he had received, the emotional appearance of his friend and the mess in the apartment.

Defense did not hold him long, but at one point tossed off the rhetorical question, "She was not a very neat housekeeper, I suppose?"

The judge took exception to offhand remarks of this nature from both sides. Defense scored with an admission that the open window looked down on a busy avenue, yet Ellen Browning had offered no scream for help.

Detective Suarez, when questioned, proved to have conducted a rather superficial investigation. He had failed to summon a fingerprint expert or a photographer to record the crime scene; nor did Suarez collect the broken pieces of glass for introduction in evidence. Had the wallet been one stolen by Elliot, the failure to search for prints might have cost the police any chance to identify the attacker. Photographs could have supported the testimony of a struggle, showing either the stained wall where the Pepsi-Cola had sloshed, or the nailed-in window screen the young woman claimed she had tried to open.

Dr. Jagdish Chandra Wadhwa's testimony furnished another critical battleground for the adversaries. He told the court, under direct examination by the prosecutor, that by its appearance the contusion on Ellen Browning's neck could not have been made more than six hours before he treated her.

"Would passion or kissing cause such a mark?"

"I object," said defense, and the court supported him, in a demand that "passion" be separated from "kissing."

The D.A. continued, "Could that [bruise] have been caused by a kiss on the neck?"

"No, no kiss is big enough to make that size mark and there were no teeth marks."

Further on, the doctor specified his techniques for taking a sample from the vaginal pool. "I placed it on a glass slide, diluted [it] with dilutant such as sodium chloride to make the sperm prominent among the debris inside the vaginal channel. Active, motile spermatozoa was demonstrable under a microscope. It was the result of recent sexual intercourse."

"Doctor," asked defense, "if a man was embracing a woman with a good deal of vigor in that area of the neck, could a bruise of that sort have been incurred?" The physician, urged on by objections from the prosecution skated away from any kind of hypothetical analysis of how the bruise might have occurred.

Defense opened up a line of attack on medical grounds, asking why no rips, bruises and tears around the vagina had been discerned. "Isn't there usually a difference between what happens to a vagina when a married female or a promiscuous female engages in intercourse?"

Again prosecution objections rang out. When the question was phrased in a less suggestive manner, the doctor was permitted to answer, "Any soft part of the body cannot cause ripping and tearing of any other parts of the body." He added that there was no way to determine whether injury would occur because of previous intercourse or lack of it.

Defense now entered into a substantial argument about the increase in vaginal secretions which accompany female orgasm and without which injury to the vagina must occur (if so, there must be tens of millions of ripped, bruised and torn vaginas in America, many of them belonging to married women as well as victims of rape who fail to reach orgasm).

The Indian-born physician rejected the defense's understanding of gynecology, insisting that a certain amount of residual fluid was always present in a woman's vagina.

While Dr. Wadwha was on the stand, a juror sent a note to the judge. "Did the examination show she was raped?" Patiently, the judge advised that that was the determination for which the jury had been assembled. Then several jurors indicated that there were questions that they would like to put to the physician. Judge Birns gently informed the panel that the case had to be tried by counsel, not by the jury.

The closing statements by both lawyers reviewed that portion of evidence favorable to their points of view while expatiating on the character of the principal witness, Ellen Browning. In particular, defense undertook to impeach her credibility. "We're not here to judge the morals and conduct of Mrs. Browning. We don't care if Mrs. Browning is the most chaste young lady that has come to New York nor do we care whether or not she's one of the most promiscuous ladies that have come to New York." He then pro-

ceeded to review her life-style in the city and concluded: "You may gather or infer that Mrs. Browning
knows her way, and in the area of sexual intercourse
it's not a strange experience to her and it certainly
wasn't strange or new to her [at the time of the
crime]." For someone who didn't care whether she
was chaste or promiscuous, defense spoke a great deal
of the matter.

Defense referred to the calls to Jeffrey Wolf and
added, "Meantime, she's carrying this culturally deprived male around with her all afternoon and
through the evening. She says this guy is a stiff, so
what is he doing with her all that time?" Defense
stressed Ellen Browning's Mississippi background,
her work for VISTA and even her testimony about her
sympathy for the hard life of black George Elliot. Defense insinuated that behind the relationship between
white woman and black man lay white guilt, white guilt
to be cleansed by an indulgence of her body. Defense
explained away the subsequent cry of rape. "This culturally deprived individual turns out to be a gorilla
and he grabs her. They got into an argument, she
called Jeffrey and told him she was raped. Probably
there was bad manners on his part or an unevenness
of appetite, or a more vigorous approach to things by
Mr. Elliot than Mrs. Browning was accustomed to.
That's her problem . . . too damn bad, we don't convict
men of serious crimes for that."

Defense dismissed the damaging evidence of the
physician with, "I'm glad he's going to practice in
India." He informed the jury that Ellen Browning had
not possessed a proper peddler's license at the time of

the incident with Elliot and bought one only afterward. It was one more effort to convince by character rather than evidence, for as defense constantly reminded the jury, "If one detail is wrong, then the whole story must be fabricated."

Prosecution strove for a less emotional tone but it too resorted to character analysis. "You saw Jeffrey Wolf [a part-time actor as well as law student] and you saw the kind of man she'd be interested in. You saw the defendant, you observed his actions, in court. You know he's a liar," a reference to Mrs. Browning's testimony that while Elliot told her he was a construction worker he was actually on welfare. When poor John Motherhill stood trial 200 years before, the prosecution also harped on the lower class, the appearance of the man who insisted the woman consented.

Judge Birns charged the jury to be aware of the rules of corroboration extant at the time of the event and it retired for deliberation. The verdict: Guilty as charged and following a probation report, Elliot received an eight-year prison term. Subsequently, it was determined that he was mentally ill and he was sent to an institution for the criminally insane.

New York v. *Elliot* demonstrates the trickiness of rape prosecution. Based upon the evidence presented to it, the jury would not have seemed irrational if it had concluded that Ellen Browning had invited attentions from Elliot and only turned against him after the act. The man did not gain entry to her apartment by force or surreptitiously. Elliot employed no weapon, Ellen Browning made no outcry. The evidence of force was all circumstantial, her disheveled appearance, complaint to Wolf, the Pepsi-Cola stains, the broken glass (so unimportant to the investigating detective that he did not include it in his report). The buttock bruise discovered by Dr. Wadwha might have been explained —just as easily—as a result of a licit hugger-mugger in bed. The mark on the neck is potentially more significant; it is less likely that a contusion could come from an embrace; lovers don't ordinarily squeeze the windpipe until the blood vessels hemorrhage. The question put by the member of the jury—did the medical examination show that the girl had been raped—only underscores the public ignorance on the anatomy of rape. A physician can, at most, describe what has happened to a body in forensic matters. He is not entitled (because he cannot, with absolute certainty) to state that an individual has been murdered; only that he died as a result of a gunshot wound, that the bullet penetrated at this point in the skull, at this angle and thus to the brain. He may confirm sexual intercourse, vaginal damage, lacerations, hematomas, contusions, cuts, bruises, scrapes, fractures but cannot conclude whether they add up to rape.

As in every trial by jury, it all melts down to a question of credibility; whom do the 12 men and women believe? There has been a surprising amount of resistance to acceptance of police testimony, particularly in New York. "They never believe us," said a frustrated sex crimes cop. This has been most particularly true in cases that have accused blacks of revolutionary or antiestablishment plots. Something of this may carry over into the rape prosecution, although flakings and dropsies, the planting of evidence on the accused by cops isn't feasible in rape cases. "You can't manufacture semen," said Lieutenant Julia Tucker, "and find the stuff at the scene of the crime. If there are no bruises or marks, you can't invent them."

Because sex figures as the hottest battleground in even the coldest war between the races, the ethnic factor, if present in any rape trial, must be recognized. A study of jury selection in three Florida counties showed that defense attorneys try to keep white women off juries for rape cases and prosecutors attempted to screen out black women. Defense believed that Southern white women are predisposed to convict for rape, while prosecution felt that rape is so commonplace in the black community the women there do not consider it worthy of elevation to the stature of a crime.

Whether the fact that Ellen Browning was white and George Elliot black played any part in the question of credibility is conjectural. Both defense and prosecution did variations on the theme. Defense pointed to her VISTA record and her description of Elliot as "culturally deprived." Prosecution contrasted the lower-class black with the "idealized" white Jeffrey Wolf. But race takes strange turns in courtrooms. "You take a black person, middle aged, who has worked all his life," said a Manhattan prosecutor, "and you will find his views on law and order as strong as a white middle-class person. What's more he or she lives in the black ghetto, and knows what's happening. I've had trials where the accused was black and the woman white or Hispanic and it was the black jurors who pushed for conviction. You get some white liberal, like I had one who was a film producer, fifty years old, trying to play Perry Mason and work off all his liberal hang-ups and it was the blacks on the jury who voted first to convict, even though the victims were all white, the accused black."

The credibility count entails factors other than race. "When you select for a jury, you have to take into account who the witnesses will be," said a D.A. "Middle-aged women may be catty about a good-looking girl who is the victim. On the other hand a man will look at a good-looking girl and feel that he would probably enjoy having sex with her and then get sore at the defendant because he not only did, but in a way that was criminal. I'm a little nervous about Hispanic men; many of them have this thing, think a man is supposed to dominate the woman. At the same time, a Hispanic man will be very tough on the defendant if he thinks of the victim in terms of his mother or his wife."

When sex crimes are brought into the courtroom, an awesome-sized double standard is unveiled. The chief witness, the victim, endures a barrage of questions about her background. Unchastity does not qualify as a defense against a rape charge but it is wholly accepted as relevant to whether or not the prosecutrix is to be believed. Defense touted the promiscuous woman theme heavily in *New York* v. *Elliot* and it is a standard number in trials for most sex crimes. It can become an incredible shriek at times. A 37-year-old Hispanic mother of three children, Juanita Correo, rode a subway train one Sunday morning on her way to a job at the telephone company in lower Manhattan. At 14th Street, several stations before her stop, a young man, Luis Aldonzo boarded the train. When she got off at her stop he followed. In a deserted corner of the station Aldonzo trapped her, intimated that he held a knife in his pocket and forced her to perform fellatio. Unsatisfied, Aldonzo led his prisoner to a truck-loading platform, hidden from the street by semitrailers. On a wooden pallet, Aldonzo mounted Mrs. Correo.

After she told her story in court, the cross-examination began. Defense began its attack with an inquiry into her clothing, hinting that a woman in a dress, girdle and pantyhose would have to assist a man. Defense targeted her marital history. "How many times have you been married?"

"Twice."

Establishing that she lived apart from her second husband and the father of her children, defense demanded, "So when I ask you if you had any relations with any other men, the answer would be, yes?" (The ability of trial lawyers to frame a question as an outright condemnation of an individual is a tribute to the subtlety of the English language if not a corruption of it.)

The attack continues with the accusation of cooperation or pleasureful compliance.

"Did you open your legs?" Another variation of the question is, "Did you move your body under him?"

During *New York* v. *Aldonzo*, defense on the occasion of the attending physician's testimony again dove into folk sexology. "It [the vagina] shows no evidence of trauma?" The doctor agreed he found no vaginal damage.

"If a woman hasn't had sexual relations for more than a full year, isn't her womb tighter and closed?"

"No."

"I am now talking about a woman, a Puerto Rican woman." When the doctor demurred that neither frequency of intercourse nor ethnic background were factors in whether trauma would necessarily result from forced intercourse, defense sneered: "Have you had experience with different women of different races?"

The judge offered some further light, "Years ago, they used to talk about the Chinese women."

Subsequently, Aldonzo was found guilty; this time a pair of black jurors led the pack in calling for a conviction.

The *New York* v. *Aldonzo* case, incidentally, demonstrated the elasticity of the law through judicial interpretation. At the time of the crime, the requirement for corroboration of identity was still in effect. The victim, Mrs. Correo, was the only person who had seen Aldonzo. However, after the cops picked him up, he admitted to them that he had boarded the subway at 14th Street at the time Mrs. Correo said he did. That "confession" was accepted by the court as tending to corroborate the witness. Aldonzo's statement did not actually place him at the site of the crime but the doctrine of the court was that the crime began at 14th Street, when he started to follow his victim. A slender thread, the connection, but in the eyes of the law, strong enough to bind Aldonzo.

The cross-examination of Mrs. Correo, as that of Ellen Browning, or for that matter most victims, struck at her chastity or lack of it. Some defense counselors steer away from impugning the reputation of the chief witness. Richard Runes of the Legal Aid Society said, "You never know how the jury will take such an approach. They might feel that the woman is being persecuted, hounded and become sympathetic." But many defenses concentrate on the reputation of the victim, and some jurisdictions insist that her good or bad name be included in the elements considered by the jury.

California, for one, demands that the judge in his charge to the jury specify that the panel may infer that a woman who has once consented to sexual intercourse would be more likely to consent again and that evidence of her unchastity goes both to the question of consent and her credibility. In addition, if the prosecutrix has lain with the accused before, that too must be weighted as further evidence of consent. To California, the woman's sex life, previous to the event in question, is highly relevant; the man's inadmissible. And at that the jury is considering as mitigating nonviolent sexual acts by the woman, it never takes into account the sexual promiscuity of the accused man as evidence of his lack of credibility.

While it is open season on the woman's reputation, a prosecutor risks a mistrial if he maneuvers to insert into the record material about the accused's previous behavior. It so happened that George Elliot had been previously named by another woman as a rapist and supposedly used the same line, "Can I use the bathroom?" to gain access. When it came time to pursue the matter, the victim decided she could not endure the trial. And only a few weeks before his encounter with Ellen Browning, he had been arrested by two cops in the midst of an assault upon a nurse that had all the earmarks of progressing to flat-out rape, but for the appearance of the law. Introduction of such information into *New York* v. *Elliot* would have demolished any defense. But generally, American jurisprudence does not allow the introduction of evidence of another sex crime by the defendant at a different time and against another person unless it may help confirm the identity of the accused. The only way to properly get any information damaging to the reputation of the accused is by cross-examining him. Defense lawyers whose client has a record naturally will keep him off the stand. As one counselor expressed it, "The more we can keep his personality out of the case, the better off we are because we don't, at least I don't, want him to become a personality to the jury."

The same lawyer, asked if he attempted to get the jury to dislike the woman answered, "yes."

Pennsylvania case law applies an evenhanded look at both principles. *Commonwealth* v. *Eberhardt*, 1949: "Evidence of bad reputation for chastity is admissable on rape charges as substantive evidence bearing on question of female's consent." *Commonwealth* v. *Ranson*, 1949, declared, "In prosecution for robbery and rape, Commonwealth was properly permitted to introduce evidence that defendants two days before alleged offenses had in another state made attempt at sexual intercourse with a chance acquaintance by use of considerable force and intimidation in order to show design."

But most prosecutors are chary of bringing in material on the reputation of the accused for fear of a mistrial or reversal on the grounds of prejudicing the actual case being tried. It is a double standard, but a trial is a criminal procedure. The civil liberties of the accused are at stake, and no one else's. Carol Halprin of the Legal Aid Society put it, "This isn't a football game where the victim somehow wins if the perpetrator goes to jail. It's not woman versus man, not her versus him, it's the people against him. It is the state attempting to deal with a problem. The criminal process includes the rights the accused should have before the state. It's not basketball, one on one. You hear due process for the complainant, but there is no such concept in the law. She is not a party to the prosecution, she is a witness."

With both prosecution and defense admitting to the irrationality of trial by jury, and both sides vigorously trading in the commodity when it appears to be bullish for them, one might suspect that a solution would be to remove sex crimes from the judgment of the peers and put it in the hands of those less ignorant, perhaps less prejudiced by irrelevancies such as race and previous behavior—the magistrates.

Legal Aid Counselor Halprin said, "I believe in juries, so much more than judges or D.A.s. I'd rather do anything, bail, motion or trial before a jury. But they can get carried away."

Judge Irving Younger who had been both a prosecutor and a defense attorney, told *New York Post* reporter Roberta Brandes Gratz, "There is a newer view about the jury which is growing but is not necessarily the prevailing view. It is that the jury is probably the only sensible part of our system for trying any kind of case. For my money it is infallible."

For the prosecution there is, of course, no point in taking a stand on juries. The state has no option when it comes to a criminal trial.

Feminists and nonideologues as well cheered as New York's corroboration requirements were removed from the penal code in 1974. But what little research exists on the subject indicates that this may prove no more efficacious in locking up the rapists than the civil-rights laws were in thrusting blacks into decent housing, better jobs, political offices or social power. The law can say what it pleases the legislators to have it say, but the jury will decide whom to believe. Given the attitudes demonstrated, jurors want more than the prosecutrix's word (except possibly in the Deep South for black on white rape, and there, too, it may be changing). Prosecutors in New York still feel that they must bring into court materials tending to show force, penetration and even identity, if it be in question.

"It may even be more difficult," said one D.A. "because now the woman may say, 'I took a shower because I knew the corroboration requirement was no longer needed.' Or she may throw out the torn night-gown because she felt we didn't need that kind of thing. And these women who make complaints do know the law, they understand why the cops have asked them for certain things. Now we'll have to convince the women that the evidence is still necessary."

One of the few—if not the only—study made of jury habits, *The American Jury* by Harry Kalven, Jr. and Hans Zeisel said that juries tend not to convict in rape trials, even if the corroboration rules have been satisfied. When it comes to sex offenses, juries do not let the facts interfere with their conclusions.

Commented the authors, "The law recognizes only one issue in rape cases other than the fact of intercourse: whether there was consent at the moment of intercourse.

"The jury, as we come to see it, does not limit itself to this issue. It goes on to weigh the woman's conduct in the prior history of the affair. It is moved to be lenient with the defendant whenever there are suggestions of contributory behavior on her part."

The MO followed by Kalven and Zeisel was to obtain from the presiding judges, their accounts of the trials. While magistrates also view evidence through their own distorting lenses, nevertheless, a judicial scan of 108 rape cases indicates jury bias based upon the doctrine of "assumption of risk," the Kalven and Zeisel term for what others label "provoked rape," or "victim precipitated." In one instance a judge reported, "The complaining witness alleged after several beers she entered a car with the defendant and three other men and was driven to a cemetery—here the act took place." The accused were all acquitted.

A second example: "The woman involved went to a public dance and was picked up by the defendant. They went to a nightclub and she permitted the defendant to take her home over an unfrequented road . . . woman involved was twice married and divorced, age thirty-three." Verdict: not guilty.

"The prosecutrix and the defendant, strangers to each other met each other at a dance hall. He undertook to take her home . . . rape occurred in a lonely wooded area, she was drinking but not drunk. He was much more under the influence." Not guilty decided the jury.

"Complaining witness and defendant were formerly married, and had two children. During [the] past year [they] had been going together . . . toward reconciliation. He spent time at prosecutrix's home. Although she denied that intercourse occurred during this period, the defendant claimed that it had." Acquitted.

The most egregious presumption of feminine unreliability by a jury considered what a judge termed "a savage case . . . [the] jaw of complaining witness was fractured in two places. The jury acquitted the defendant on the basis of testimony that they had been out together before, and had been drinking on the evening in question. The defendant claimed he'd had intercourse with her prior to occurrence."

Character overwhelmed the evidence in other instances. "Three men kidnapped a girl off the street at one-thirty A.M., took her to [an] apartment and attacked her. Defense showed she had two illegitimate children. Defense also claimed she was a prostitute, although no evidence beyond the word of the defendant on this was introduced." Again, the verdict was not guilty.

Given the opportunity to find the accused guilty of a lesser crime, rape juries tended to go that route. If it was either first-degree rape or acquittal, the trend went toward not guilty. Based on this admittedly sketchy research, the "lock 'em up and throw away the key" school might ponder the potential results of tougher penalties. As far back as John Motherhill, juries, when faced with either Draconian measures or permissiveness, have opted for the latter.

In aggravated rape, where the violence went beyond just threats and the sexual act itself, juries in the Kalven and Zeisel book showed much more willingness to convict. Judges found themselves in disagreement only 12 percent of the time. But in simple rape, the magistrates hearing the evidence along with the veniremen, would have convicted 60 percent more of the time. Rapists ordinarily would be well-advised not to waive trial by jury if accused of a sexual offense in which the victim's only injury was emotional.

Although the judges, or at least those who presided over the trials surveyed by Kalven and Zeisel, showed far more willingness to find the accused guilty, the sentences handed out by judges to convicted rapists is another contentious subject. A New York City summary of first-degree sex offense cases (rape, attempted rape, and sodomy in the first degree) in the first six months of 1972, broke down 647 arrests in the period. Of these, 290 were reduced to misdemeanors (of which 2 men received jail terms of a year and another

13 served a maximum of 8 months). The grand jury took on 323 cases, dismissed 110 and indicted the other 213. At the end of the criminal justice maze, 92 men were convicted but less than half, 42, went to prison. The statistics shook down to 10 men with an under one-year rap, 19 on a 1–5 years, 11 men given 6–25 and a pair with indefinite stays on the state.

California's 1967 investigation of its disposition of convicted rapists produced the same sort of picture, 15.2 percent of the convicted rapists disappeared into the slammer, where they were joined, for example, by 43.2 percent of those convicted of robbery. However, would-be rapists would be well-advised to steer clear of Connecticut. In the two years from July 1, 1970 to June 30, 1972, the superior court locked up 80 percent of its rapists (the length of stays was not published). Still, when it came to burglarly, better than 85 percent of the Connecticut thieves after conviction, became cell bound.

Possibly a prize for irrational sentencing should have gone to Alaskan judges in *State* v. *Chaney*. As described by Camille LeGrande in the *California Law Review*, the evidence showed that Donald Chaney, an off-duty soldier, and a companion invited a woman into their automobile whereupon they raped her four times, forced her to commit fellatio, stole her money and threatened her with reprisals if she went to the police. The facts of the occurrence were not in dispute on the appeal, only the sentence. A military spokesman who appeared on behalf of Chaney, told the sentencing court, "An occurrence such as the one concerned here is very common and happens many times each night in Anchorage. Needless to say, Donald Chaney was the unlucky G.I. that picked a young lady who told."

On the strength of that oration, and, perhaps, the fact that Chaney was in the service of his country, the trial judge gave him two concurrent one-year terms and urged immediate parole.

The prosecution appealed the slap on the wrist sentence. In its review Alaska's Supreme Court noted that the defendant never showed any remorse for his acts, and it criticized the trial court for treating him as though "he was only technically guilty and minimally blameworthy." It ordered a stiffer penalty imposed. But even at that the Alaska Supreme Court judges felt obliged to back up the lower court's perception of the victim's voluntary entrance into the defendant's car as mitigating circumstances that properly should go toward reduction of sentence.

What the law giveth, the law can take away. If it can stretch the thinnest material to cover the most massive outreaches of the penal code rules, it can also blind itself to fact through outrageous prejudice.

IX

Where It's Not At

Where it's not at:

Susan Brownmiller, in an interview in *Esquire*, stated that: "Rape is to woman what lynching was to black men in the South. I formulated the phrase, 'Rape is a political crime against women.' It was the most exciting new idea that had ever entered my consciousness." (The woman as nigger, the student as nigger, it must comfort all the real niggers to know so many others feel themselves similarly abused.)

With typical male chauvinism, it has been said that the success has a thousand fathers, and failure none (at least nobody blamed it on a mother). For the notion that rape is a political crime, there are a number of maternal claimants. But catchy phrases are not a test of truth. To make rape the equivalent of lynching makes no sense. The purpose of lynch law was to keep the black man from entering the mainstreams of commerce, government and social standing. It was a punishment meted out to those who transgressed the white man's idea of law. Rape does not prevent women from economic, governmental or social accession. Rape is nonselective; it does not focus on uppity women. Rape is most frequently committed upon poor black females by black men.

Politics, turning again to Noah Webster, deals first with the science or art of government. A rape is no more a political act than a simple mugging. Neither crime ordinarily concerns itself with the effect on the victim or others. Unlike a lynching, they're committed solely for the gain of the perpetrators. In another interview, Brownmiller assaulted Eldridge Cleaver for his attempt to make rape a revolutionary act. "That's absolutely not acceptable and has even been repudiated by Bobby Seale. Cleaver goes into great detail about how he practiced on black women before raping whites, which is just another example of the property concept of women." Had Susan Brownmiller read page 15, as well as page 14, of *Soul on Ice* she would have seen that Cleaver himself had repudiated rape: "After I returned to prison, I took a long look at myself, and for the first time in my life, admitted that I was wrong, that I had gone astray—astray not so much from the white man's law as from being human, civilized—for I could not approve the act of rape. Even though I had some insight into my own motivations, I did not feel justified, I lost self-respect. My pride as a man dissolved and my whole fragile moral structure seemed to collapse, completely shattered." It must be admitted that the Black Panthers made themselves an easy target for feminists when a spokesman answered the question, "What's the proper position for women," with "Prone." The designated position has since been repudiated.

The act of rape is simply one more example of the all-too-human resort to force by the physically stronger to procure something desired from the weaker. It is as political as a barroom argument in which the blockhead achieves acquiesence by punching out his punier adversary. There are much more sophisticated and effective means to oppress women than rape which, at most, is only a symptom of certain attitudes about women.

A mugger does not launch an assault upon a 275-pound defensive tackle from a professional team. That is not a political decision; it is recognition that one stands to get the shit beat out of him for such an attack.

"In the spectrum of male behavior, rape, the perfect combination of sex and violence, is the penultimate act [the author does not grant us knowledge of the ultimate act]. Though the law attempts to make a clear division between rape and sexual intercourse, in fact the courts find it difficult to distinguish between a case where the decision to copulate was mutual and where a man forced himself upon his partner. . . .

"According to the double standard, a woman who has had sexual intercourse out of wedlock cannot be raped. Rape is not only a crime of aggression against the body; it is a transgression against chastity as defined by men. When a woman is forced into a sexual relationship, she has, according to the male ethos, been violated. But she is also defiled if she does not behave according to the double standard, by maintaining her chastity, or confining her sexual activities to a monogamous relationship." This comes from "Rape, the All-American Crime" by Susan Griffin, *Ramparts* magazine, and, according to *The New Woman's Survival Guide* edited by Kirsten Grimstad and Susan Rennie, "the first, and is still the best, statement exposing the political implications of rape."

But courts don't have any "trouble" separating a case where the decision to copulate was mutual and where a man forced himself upon his partner. The problem is to determine whether or not the decision *was* mutual, whether or not there was consent. The courts damn well know what rape is but the problem is to prove it to the satisfaction of a jury of peers, we the people, we the men and women—not of some abstraction called a court. One can argue that many rapists have escaped punishment because defense conveyed to the jury that the chief witness has had intercourse out of wedlock. But don't tell that to George Elliot, moldering in a New York prison.

Writing in "Violence and the Masculine Mystique," Lucy Komisar states: "The ultimate proof of manhood is in sexual violence. . . . Men are aggressive as they take or make women, showing their potency (power) in the conquest. Women on the other hand, submit and surrender, allowing themselves to be violated and possessed. Havelock Ellis declares the basic sadomasochism of such a concept to be certainly normal." Anyone who still uses the words "normal" or "abnormal" to describe psychological states of mind ought to be sentenced to read the collected works of Havelock Ellis including the seven volumes on the *Psychology of Sex.*

"Closing the male/female split means a drastic rearrangement of the barriers between the weak and the powerful. Then not women, but the weak, become the second sex, subordinate, submissive, subject to rape.

"Alliance with women removes from men the protection of maleness against rape by the powerful; and though, in our society, the fear of rape by men of men is not often acknowledged, it exists. James Dickey's novel *Deliverance* tapped that fear and gained great force by so doing. The premise underlying this fear is quite clear: if power has no bounds, it will extend to physical misuse. The paradigmatic act of the powerful, performed upon the weak is rape.

"Now rape need not always be performed by force. In fact, one of the charms of pornography is that it records session after session of guiltless rape in which the powerful are licensed to have their will of the weak because the weak 'really like it that way' "—from "The Weak Are the Second Sex," by Elizabeth Janeway, *Harper's* magazine.

For the sake of Ms. Janeway's argument I'll accept her nonlegal assumption of rape as applicable to males. It's my guess (and as a man I think I'm in a better position to guess than she is, I do not assert any ability to climb into the collective mind of womenkind) that the male fear of rape exists largely in the confines of a prison or some other restricted male populations. Otherwise it's about as strong as the fear of being consumed by a shark. If I fell overboard in the South

Pacific sharks would come to mind, and if I were in a prison I might worry about a homosexual attack. Dickey chose his approach because it was plausible for the milieu and plot; others rely on fear of flying, the Irish Republican Army, Satan or a large white whale. Certainly power that has no bounds extends to physical misuse. But rape is the paradigmatic act of the powerful only because Ms. Janeway says so. If I could take my pick of the paradigmatics (such words seduce reason), I'd take genocide.

When we get down to rape, she says it need not always be performed by force. Janeway has arrived in Wonderland; words now mean what I say they mean. Just so, an invasion becomes an incursion, a murder becomes termination with extreme prejudice and a fake protest becomes a political hardball. Rape without force. Yes, and there's ham and eggs without ham. You can call it bacon and eggs, but there's no ham and eggs without ham. On the legal menu, there's rape, there's seduction and there's prostitution. You don't have one if you have the other: No substitutions, please.

Omniverous ideologies get bellyaches trying to devour the indigestible. And it does no good to slop some fancy sauce over the concept. Rape is obnoxious, but instead of being dignified as some sophisticated political weapon it ought to be known for the dirty little terror that it is, a result of the social organization, not a mechanism of it. That cops, doctors and we the people, the men and the women, don't see rape for what it is, does not change its nature. Lincoln supposedly once asked a man if he were to call a dog's tail a leg, how many legs would the dog have? The straight man answered five, of course. No, said Lincoln, calling a tail a leg doesn't make it a leg. And calling rape political doesn't change its nature.

Ms. Griffin served up a morsel with genuine meat, however, when she called rape "a transgression against chastity." She obscured it, however, with some unnecessary verbiage in her qualification, "as defined by man." But chastity is at the epicenter of the rape configuration. Chastity, and its sibling, virginity, have been basic values of Judeo-Christian Western tradition. They have been honored as one of the birth rights to the female. The worth of a small, basically, nonfunctional piece of tissue, the hymen, remains high, even today. In Sicily, should a male deflower a woman, even against her will, he wins the right to wed her. The vagina itself does not erode with use.

Chastity as a value undoubtedly owes its existence to its ancient function, the affirmation of parentage. The woman can be certain the child grew from her egg; the man could not then, cannot today possess the certainly that the seed was nourished by his sperm. Why was it felt necessary to determine parentage? Among a nomadic people the issue of who was responsible for whom was paramount. Stability for the group, the orderly transmission of culture and tradition could be sustained, particularly in the face of threats from outside the group. The concept's origins survive in modern Israel. Who is a Jew depends entirely upon the maternal line. Children born to an Israeli man of impeccable Jewish lineage and his Protestant wife who now professed to be of no religion were declared not

Jewish in the celebrated Shalit case. At the heart of the *contretemps* lay the tradition that blood lines remain intact, for sure, only through the female. Chastity is the means to insure the identity of a child.

Polygamy has always centered around one man and many wives. It is explicable in the absence of birth control, the time necessary for gestation and the need of a society to expand its membership. Still, even in polygamous groupings, the identity of parentage depended upon chastity.

Some have sought to explain the origins of chastity as the property concept of women. But the proscriptions against unchastity predate the sanctification of mine and yours. Private property was not part of the old Hebrews' bag and the Biblical ancients inveighed against both rape and unchastity. When the idea of private property did take hold, it blended with chastity neatly. A man could insure the parentage of his own offspring by keeping his wife literally or figuratively locked up while enjoying a free-fire zone for his own sexual pleasure. And, of course, practices that start out as functional eventually take on a ritualistic value as well. Witness the need to avoid trichinosis which led to the Hebrew practice of forbidding pork—part of keeping kosher. Today, the pig is as healthy as the steer or chicken, but the ritual of kosher remains. Therefore, even where there is no question of an offspring or its lineage, thanks to contraception, surgery or abortion, the ritual value of chastity continues to plague women. Traditions that have thousands of years behind them die hard. Men who wrote the laws, made up the courts that pursued their advantage.

They have abused the once honorable purpose of chastity. That, however, does not make rape a political crime, simply one more example of man's inhumanity to woman.

For that matter, the chastity complex has been one of the tough obstacles for female consciousness-raising to overcome. Women jurors bring to court the same obsessions with chastity as men. There is no evidence that females more readily convict accused rapists than do males. Note how often victims felt themselves "unclean" or talked of "guilt." Some psychiatrists blame the chastity bit for female fantasies of rape. "It is a way for a woman to see herself in a sexual situation without any guilt for her behavior. She was forced."

Psychoanalyst Helene Deutsch, not without support among the professionals and male laity, put it all on innate masochism in women: "What the woman ultimately wants in intercourse is to be raped and violated, that only if she experienced sex as rape could she avoid frigidity." Like any drug, chastity has its secondary effects. It implies that a woman take a passive role in sexual expression which translates into playing hard to get. The stage is set for the great miscalculation. Does she really mean no, or just desire more ardent wooing. How the hell was I to know that you were just being maidenly (at least no legal crime has been committed by my timidity)? Or, how the hell was I to know that you really meant no?

While it would seem obvious to some when she means no, the irrationality of the sex drive fuzzes perceptions. *Homo sapiens erectus* loses his ability to make fine distinctions. Sex is a volatile element; that is not an excuse but it should be a warning like the sign that says "danger, high voltage." Both men and women ought to be sensitive to the potential of sexually charged situations.

Elevated consciousness of the nature of rape has been slowed by another somewhat sinister movement in America. It is hinted at by the very existence of the new science, victimology, by terms like "victim precipitated" or "victim provoked." The idea is not restricted to social crimes. Victim-precipitated homicide is also on the drawing boards of behavioral scientists.

Once upon a time, when Hollywood depicted organized crime, the legitimate businessmen, the decent people, were shown as being oppressed by the Mob. Now, a la Godfather, the only people that the Mafia dumps on are loathsome in themselves. The victims we see deserve what they get. The Jews who went to the ovens might have escaped if they had been better Jews. The blacks in the ghetto earned their right to be living on that level. When white sociologists like Daniel Moyniham look at racism, they turn their attention on the black family, the black woman, the black teenager. You learn all about black sociopathology, not white society's. Robert Sherrill in *The Saturday Night Special*, while ruminating over the large number of Americans who expire annually by gunshot, remarked that most of them were not very solid citizens anyway. Even the soggy excuses vouchsafed for Watergate conduct, "everybody does it," "they did things like this in other campaigns," are one more attempt to make the victim guilty.

Rape and what to do about it has become a prime topic for women's groups in recent years. There have been speakouts at which victims have come forward to tell of their experiences, their difficulties with the cops, the physicians, the law and their own heads. In the absence of much institutional help, rape crisis centers have been formed across the country. Volunteers in as many as 25 cities offer counseling to victims, offer to accompany them to court, attempt to inform the public, work to improve official treatment of victims, lobby for law changes. Such groups can take credit for changes in the law on corroboration in New York, improved cooperation from hospitals in Philadelphia, and better treatment by the cops in both Philadelphia and Berkeley.

Many of the women's groups stress the need to fight back, to learn how to resist through classes in karate and other martial arts. "Chop at his throat (especially his Adam's apple) or across his nose with the side of your hand." "Jab him in the eyes, using your first two fingers as prongs." It has also been suggested that a woman stick her fingers down her throat in an attempt to turn off the aroused male with her gush of vomit. She can also try defecating at a tactically auspicious moment.

While physical resistance, even screams, may drive an attacker off, and a black belt provides a certain sense of well-being and security, most police experts are dubious about the womanly art of self-defense. To resist an armed attacker may be ideologically right, but personally damned dangerous. "Our first rule," said a cop, "is that if a man has a weapon on you, it's better to give him what he wants." The number of homicides that have resulted after a householder surprised a would-be burglar, who then panicked during a struggle or because his escape was blocked is depressing. Self-defense schools with a hard sell on how the 110-pound woman beats off the 180-pound brute fail to recognize the paralysis due to the intruder's sudden presence or the potential of the adversary. "You are dealing with a very unstable situation," said Dr. Peters recently in his appraisal of resistance. The rapist has apparently already crossed the border line from lawful to unlawful. His reaction to resistance is incalculable. A nearby kitchen knife, a heavy ashtray, his fists, can totally stun a woman.

The right of a woman to say no is unquestioned. But to insist better dead than bed defies even the logic of the situation. Forcible rape by definition means without consent (as Martha Eames remembered), if consciousness-raising counts for anything, without guilt. To resist and to risk bloody hell means sanctifying the shibboleth of chastity, that the circumstances of the intercourse mean nothing, the fact is everything. It insures that if the villains accomplish their purpose the women must feel they have done wrong, that they are spiritually as well as physically dirty.

On the other hand, when the victim knows her attacker well enough to be certain that there are limits to his reaction, a sharp chop on the nose bridge or a kick in the testicles may be in order.

The most constructive efforts have been in the areas of treatment by authorities, public information and the necessity for women to come forward. Martha Eames may be correct in her perception of the cops coming on to her. But this could be changing. An assistant D.A. in Manhattan said, "I've investigated 66 charges of rape and in only one of these did I hear a complaint about the cops." Hospitals around the country still lag in their perception of the needs of victims. Washington, D.C.'s Women Against Rape bitterly criticized the treatment accorded victims there. Bay Area Women Against Rape discovered that the San Francisco-Oakland hospitals had been given a paper by a physician on proper care of a rape victim in which the language was outrageously sexist. For several years officials of New York City hospitals have talked vaguely of special facilities, but nothing has gone beyond the planning stage, despite the urging of the likes of Dr. Clark Smith, head of Emergency Services at Brooklyn's Greenpoint Hospital and the Williamsburgh-Greenpoint Comprehensive Health Planning Board.

What Dr. Smith seeks is federal funding for a staff of psychiatric and social workers. But the federal health planners prefer to think in terms of funding hardware rather than services. Dr. Peters, who had a tough fight to get moneys for his project, compared the willingness of the feds to cough up millions to buy cops armored cars, riot guns and electronic gear. "For rape," said Dr. Peters, "I suppose I might have gotten a better response if I had asked for money to buy chastity belts."

In New York, women believe they have won a mighty victory with the abolition of the corroboration requirements in the courts. But in the eyes of a D.A. who is quite friendly toward the feminist position, it will not result in a dramatic increase in the number of convictions. The sticking point for rape remains the public attitude, a long-term project of education.

The kind of rape that puts everyone up most tightly is the assault, sometimes brutal, by a stranger who comes down the fire escape or seizes the woman on the street. In these instances, what is defined by law as corroboration amounts to clues for the police. Only through what a court would call corroboration can the perpetrator be identified and apprehended, and more than likely proven guilty beyond a reasonable doubt. Rewriting the statutes will not have any significant effect upon this segment of rapes. An absence of strictures on corroboration will, however, make it easier to prosecute the case where the accused was known by his alleged victim and where he left no evidence of his attack.

Some protests broke out after an individual, free on bail while accused of rape, was collared for a subsequent rape murder. Demonstrators petitioned for higher bonds for rape suspects. The theoretical purpose of bail is to guarantee appearance in court. Excessive bail serves as preventive detention. Possibly everyone accused of crimes against people, stickup men, muggers and rapists, ought to undergo psychiatric examination to determine whether their release on bond constitutes a continued danger to other human beings. That would be counter to civil libertarian values, a step toward behavior modification enterprises with all of their hideous potentialities. But to single out rapists for such special treatment or preventive detention is to return rape to a special category of crime, something that women have only begun to free it from.

Getting women to come forward to press charges would get rapists off the street, give pause to some potential offenders. Unfortunately, some women may be discouraged because of the information programs by women against rape, broadsides that focus on the unpleasant experiences. Heavy stress on abominable behavior by the cops and the rigors of the courtroom intimidates prospective witnesses rather than spurs them onward. A district attorney remarked to me, "I'd appreciate it if you would not indicate that a trial is an ordeal. We don't want to see it made any tougher to get victims to pursue the case." I would have liked to oblige, but as the procedure stands now, testifying in a criminal case, any criminal matter, but certainly rape, extracts a price. As long as we have the adversary system of justice, defense is going to take its licks at impeaching the credibility of hostile witnesses. Support for witnesses ought to be a major role for women's groups.

What to do about the guilty parties continues to puzzle. Stiffer sentences, in crime after crime, do not seem to have much effect upon offenders. They only make juries less willing to convict. One partial explanation for London's comparatively low number of rapes is that it is one of only two offenses which carry life imprisonment, the most severe punishment under

British law. As a result, sociologists perceive a reluctance to proceed on rape, if some other crime can be charged. The Washington, D.C. Task Force on Rape specifically recommended that the penalty for rape be *lowered* to bring it in line with other sentences for crimes against a person.

Some feel it would be profitable to administer psychiatric treatment to sexual offenders. But U.S. penitentiaries show little inclination to become engines of rehabilitation. In addition, no one seems to be sure of what ails the sex criminal. If rape is a political crime then perhaps the perpetrators ought to attend classes in civics. But what if rape rises out of the volatile chemical mix of biology and environment. And if, as the preliminary data shows, recidivism among rapists is so low, why bother with any kind of therapy at all except for the most obviously psychotic.

Susan Griffin concluded, "No simple reforms can eliminate rape. As the symbolic experience of the white male hierarchy, rape is the quintessential act of our civilization, one which Valerie Solanis warns is in danger of 'humping itself to death.' " Poetry and philosophy have again overtaken reason. The opening declarative is the kind of truism upon which everyone agrees and then is swiftly ignored. Police behavior or judicial disposition are basically what the women's groups against rape hope to change and these fall under the heading of simple reforms. An efficiently operating prepaid medical plan makes entrance into a hospital easy. But it does not cure the cancer eating at the vitals. Procedural reforms that ease some of the friction of the criminal justice system do not significantly lower the rates of murder, drug addiction, robbery. And far more than sexism, these affronts are rape's affinities.

Laying it all on the white male hierarchy fits the philosophical overkill of a consistent politically extreme position but it falls apart under scrutiny. Black men rape also and unless one succumbs to the nonsense that the male black is the white man's instrument against women, the proposition is half-flawed. It's the quintessential act according to Susan Griffin; it was the paradigmatic one for Elizabeth Janeway. But depending upon whether one is an ecology freak, a survivor of the Nazi Final Solution, a black ghetto kid or a rape victim, the symbol for what ails us is a matter of choice. As for Valerie Solanis's interpretation, a number of equally qualified authorities might suggest that the real problem is too little humping.

Still, there lingers in all of these explanations of rape a seed of truth. Rape is one microcosm of human relations. Whether it is a heterosexual relationship, a homosexual one, a parent and child, boss and employee, black and white, male and female, the structure of society is at fault through the institutions that exploit and frustrate, that bring rage against others. Closest to the crime, a new assessment of sexual values is in order. Some say that total sexual freedom, coupling on demand, or at least desire, would eliminate forcible rape. However, the number of hookers on the street has never been greater. The barriers to sexual expression never been lower, and yet rape continues. (Other lands with similarly open sexuality do not have the same high incidence of rape; therefore, "permissiveness" cannot be blamed either.) To make the sexual connection a thing of no value puts it on the same level as masturbation, which is easier to accomplish, you need only yourself. Until shown otherwise, I have to think that the sexual connection is the strongest building block for relationships between adult humans. And if we are to survive, if from two to six billion are to last on this planet, we need those relationships.

On the other hand, the exclusivity that goes under the name of chastity can't be allowed to reach such a price level that its loss, under whatever circumstances, bankrupts the victim. It's those abstract values like chastity that destroy us. The one called "honor" cost the United States 50,000 men in Vietnam, to say nothing of what it did to the local people. An assault upon a woman ought not to demean her worth in either her own eyes or those of her associates. Whenever chastity gets exalted over living, breathing women, victims become burdened with a sense of guilt even if they have been faultless. It's everybody's business to balance out the sexual values.

Whether the offense itself can ever be totally eliminated is questionable. But along with concern for the victims must go a search for a cure for the "madness" in some men. So far all we can be certain of is that the crime of rape won't be halted by more prisons, more cops, female chauvinist statements. Like the woman said, "no simple reforms."